SCATTERED

Legacy Road Publishing

Joyce Ackermann

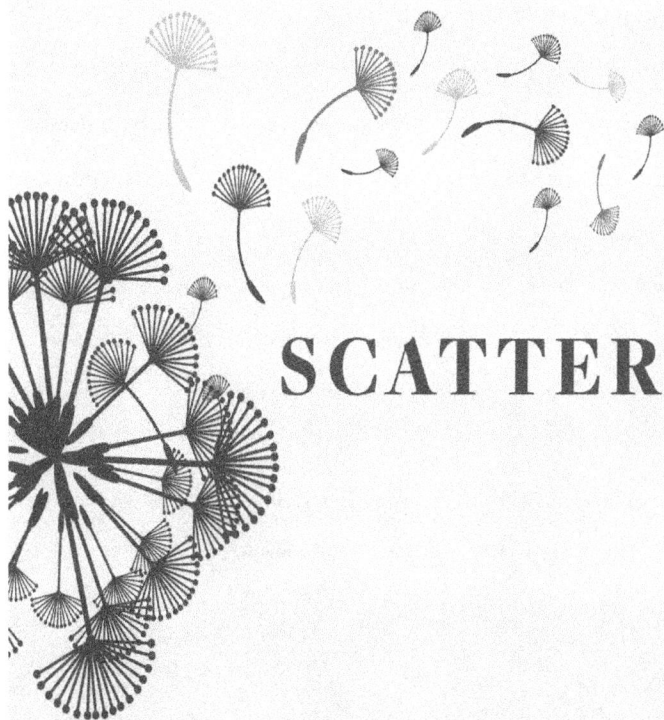

SCATTERED

FINDING GOD IN
YOUR STORY

ISBN: 978-0692719923

Photo Credit © 2016 Rebekah Bye – www.simplicityink.com

Cover Design © 2016 by Clement Vaccaro – www.clementvaccaro.com

In loving dedication to Jason, who taught me that it was okay to just be; to just breathe. Also to my dad, my hero. I still have your letters. And to my other Father, who protected me every step of the journey. It seems cliché to thank You for so lovingly penning the story of my life. My prayer and hope is that my life will echo my overwhelming gratitude with every sentence I write, every word I speak, and every life I touch.

CONTENTS

1

Bleh

Throwing Up with Words

The thing about writing is – there really are no rules in the beginning, except one.

Just write.

The temptation is to overanalyze or criticize.

You're not in it for anyone but you at this point.

The idea is to just get the raw emotion out.

It's a lot like throwing up.

After my husband and I first got married, we went to a fondue restaurant.

It was awesome, except when it wasn't.

Which was about an hour after we got home.

We both had gotten food poisoning.

For the next 24 hours we took turns tossing our cookies, - - er, fondue.

We would roll over and gently rub one another's backs and say encouraging things like, "I'm sorry babe, it'll be o – o – ohhhhhh no, Where's the bucket?"

Romantic huh?

That's kinda what I had in mind when I started writing.

Throwing up that is, not romance.

I had been poisoned by some things that had happened to me as a child and I just needed to get it out.

Hence, the figurative "Bleh" all over my laptop.

I would have Oscar-winning rants; all while sipping joe and jamming out to Goo Goo Dolls. It was messy, it was painful, and in the end – it was healing.

I would look up new words to express things like sad and mad. And later, I expanded my writing to include phrases that expressed deeper emotions . . . like – "really sad" and "really mad".

And there was a beautiful clarity that began to form as I wrote. . . I was a hot mess.

When I started writing ten years ago, I was really emotionally damaged.

As in, I made train wrecks look good.

But I heard God speak to me. It was only one word at the time, "write".

I think I responded dumbly with an "uh, okay."

Really though, what are you supposed to say when God tells you something like that?

"No?"

And so began my journey of Bleh.

I cried and bled for the art of it all.

Facing painful memories and hoping for answers.

After a couple of years, it was there – my art of "Bleh" in black and white. And it looked something like a Van Gogh.

My life splashed on a typeset canvas.

Except no one liked me well enough to buy my art of "Bleh", but on the other hand I didn't hate it enough to cut off any body parts – you know, like an ear or something.

More years passed and I began to value what had been slowly happening to my life through something as simple as writing.

Old wounds that never seemed to heal were finally beginning to scar over.

I wasn't as scared of letting my walls down and letting people in to see me in all of my vulnerability. My relationships with others began to heal, I began to value myself, and my perception of God took on new lenses.

So this is my story, and I hope that by the end of this journey, you'll find that it's okay to share yours.

Because your story is worth telling.

To help heal your own heart as much as lend courage to someone else, who may just be in the very place that you have once been.

....

I pushed open the door and was greeted by a petite girl at the counter.

"The usual?" she asked as she effortlessly flipped her wispy, blonde hair to the side.

"Yeah, that would be great." I said as I pushed a wrinkled five dollar bill towards her across the counter. "Keep the change," I said over my shoulder, as I walked to the high top table next to the wall. Sweet familiarity – my table, my coffee, my corner of the world. I shrugged my canvas briefcase off of my shoulder and unzipped the case.

As I unloaded my relic of a laptop with a thud on the table, a sing-songy voice called me back to the counter, "white mocha with a shot of caramel an' hazelnuuuuut."

A creature of coffee comforts and habits, I always ordered the same drink, a white mocha with a shot of caramel and a shot of hazelnut – full shots. I'm not sure what to name it, – the jury's still out on that one, but I've been thinking a nice throw back to the 80's might be in order with a name like the M.C. Hazelnut or maybe something sassy like "the Minq", my nickname from high school, which is short for moody chink.

Now might be a good time to throw in a disclaimer. Asians, or at least the ones I know, love to make Asian jokes.

Seriously.

We view it as a perk of being, well, a perk of being Asian.

I sat down at the table I usually sat at, like I said, creature of comfort and habit, and nursed my warm, sugary concoction while soaking in the cabiny feel of the coffee shop. Pine planks lined the walls and amateur photographs of North American wildlife hung above every table. A fireplace and a children's play area were tucked away in the corner, complete with fuzzy bear footrests. I turned my attention towards the front door to see that there was a steady stream of customers coming through, ready to order the usual cup of evening Joe.

I took another sip of coffee and shifted my focus to my laptop. I frowned at the screen, not really knowing where to start.

"Who am I?" I mouthed at the blinking cursor on my Word document.

I drummed my fingers on the well worn table top. My entire life had been defined by a woman I barely knew.

"Sigh."

Could someone just rewind it all? I wanted a do-over for this thing called life. Suddenly, I felt old – like I had lived too long. Twenty-five and way past my expiration date like the forgotten milk in the back of my fridge.

I reigned my unbridled thoughts away from my neglected and possibly curdled, dairy product and breathed in the nutty, comforting aroma of the coffee shop. I mindlessly traced the checkered design on the table.

"What now, God?" I wondered. "You said, 'Write,' so this is me, trying to write."

There was still so much I wanted to do with my life, but here I was twenty-five and well-worn. And yet, there was such a big world out there. Surely, there was still a life for me to live out there in it. I still had dreams, not moth-eaten by time or the nay-sayers. That had to count for something. I had held my precious dreams so close, close enough to protect them. And yet, managed to hold them at arm's length, afraid to be disappointed by their fragility. I rested my fingers on the keys and aimlessly stared out the window at the inky night.

···

I stared out the window into the darkness holding my stuffed raccoon as we left our home and drove south towards an unknown future. I nuzzled my cheek against the soft fur and pushed my oversized, steel-framed glasses up onto my nose. It was quiet, just the hum of the motor and the tires against the asphalt. I closed my eyes and pondered the questions that a six year old girl and her stuffed raccoon had no answers to.

"What will our new home be like?"

"Will life change for the better?"

*"Would **she** be better?"*

Alaska was the last place that felt like home. It was a confusingly, magical place where the sun didn't set until the hidden hours of the morning. And in this very same place, the sun would only dare to poke its bashful head out for a few bleak hours each day during the remainder of the year. Harsh climates were tempered only by the breathtaking landscapes. It was a place where imagination and reality were one in the same. A place that had poetic names, like Rainbow Trout, for a shiny gray fish and the Iditarod, for a really long sled race. It was the place that taught me the importance of heeding the instruction "do not stick your tongue to the flagpole". In fact, I recall learning that lesson several times.

11

Alaska's reputation was built from the things that made it unpredictable, current-fighting salmon, majestic mountains and the lakes, clear as crystal. It was an unfettered land, where man and beast alike shared an appreciation for the peace and tranquility that only a place so pure could offer. A place where the land grew wild and bent men's wills to build around itself rather than through it.

A place that could have been a home, but laughter did not fill our house and our rooms did not contain wonderful family traditions. Our bookshelves were not cluttered with meaningful heirlooms nor were our hallways lined with poignant family portraits. Sweet memories were scarce in my house. . . .

We all just wanted to forget.

It was this place that we drove mile by mile away from.

....

I sighed again and pushed my laptop towards the center of the table and absent mindedly sipped my mocha while trying to stifle the rising emotions about my childhood. Somewhere I heard that journaling was supposed to be cleansing for the soul. I have to think that whoever came up with that brilliant piece of psycho-babble never really had much to write. If they did, it was nowhere near as excruciating as what I felt at this present moment. I was willing myself to undergo a surgery of the soul, but somehow it felt like the anesthetic had worn off already and I was only 5 minutes into the procedure.

....

That year we packed up and drove the scenic route to Fort Rucker, Alabama. We had packed only the necessities into the red, Toyota truck. Everything else was coming in delivery trucks later. My stuffed raccoon and I sat in the back while my mother and dad sat in the front.

13

We stopped often.

We saw the Black Hills and Custer's Last Stand. My dad being a rabid, history buff was ecstatic. He had been looking forward to seeing Custer's Last Stand for years. Unfortunately, we didn't stay long, my mother wanted to leave.

....

"Fifteen minutes 'til closing," the blonde said aloud to whomever was listening. I picked up my belongings and walked out to my car, lost in a sea of my mind numbing emotions. Maybe if this writing thing didn't pan out I could get a job making M.C. Hazelnuts – it seemed a lot less painful.

....

It was a diner in the Black Hills that became the final resting place for my stuffed raccoon; he was my security blanket, my best and only friend. I must have brought him into the diner and forgot to bring him with me when we loaded back into the truck.

It was a foreshadowing of things to come.

Nothing would be secure or safe again.

2

Cyborgs & Origami

What's Wrong with Me?

You know those obnoxious people with reasons for a whole lotta don't and too afraid to do.

That was me.

At least, I'm pretty sure that was me.

My wiring was different then, so it's hard to remember these kinds of things.

I used to hide behind the safety of being a good Christian and was scared that God would find out I wasn't the spiritual cyborg I had hoped I was.

Don't knock it, cyborgs are very cool.

It's just not a great idea to live your life that way.

Problem was, I was really good at being a cyborg.
I followed all of my religious programming flawlessly.

But underneath it all, there was a glitch.

I didn't do anything wrong because I was too afraid to.

And I know that I sound like I'm five right now, but it's true.

I was afraid that God would stop loving me.

I wasn't entirely sure that he loved me in the first place.

But after going back and trying to make sense of this life that I was writing about, I was beginning to feel less like an indestructible cyborg and more like a discarded piece of origami.

Fold here.

Fold there.

Crease.

Viola!

You have a crane.

Except the paper crane went horribly wrong.

It looked more like Darth Vader's ship from that Star Wars movie. You know, the one with all of those cute little Ewoks running around with spears.

And thinking of Darth Vader reminded me of God.

And thinking of God reminded me that he had left me.

Which left me to wonder, "What is wrong with me?"

He had abandoned me.

Left me alone to figure out how to fold the paper to make the crane whole again.

God?

Why did you leave?

Where were you when I needed you?

SCATTERED

···

*I walked into the familiar coffee shop and found my usual
table. I ordered an M.C. Hazelnut, switched on my laptop, and
stared at my screen as it flickered impatiently at me. I fiddled with
the brown, corrugated sleeve around my cup. Even chatting with a
blank sheet of paper on a computer felt invasive, but then again, I
had never been good about baring my soul to anyone.*

*I lifted my eyes from my unsympathetic computer screen and
nervously glanced around the shop, feeling as though I had shared
my thoughts aloud. The faint sounds of paper rustling caught my
attention and out of the corner of my left eye, saw an elderly
gentleman sitting on the leather couch in the corner, meticulously
folding his newspaper.*

*My vision panned across to a couple giggling quietly at a
nearby table. I watched the two of them as they sat forehead to
forehead, whispering, their fingers intertwined with one another.
My eyes lingered on the scene as it played out before me. The man
gently swept a single strand of her auburn hair from her forehead. I*

smiled and looked away feeling a bit too voyeuristic, but grateful for the reminder that life was still good.

Despite the heartache and horror of this life, there was still good.

....

"You know, it's funny really," I paused collecting my thoughts. I inhaled the night air deeply, as if the memories of my childhood would come to me on it. "I've always known that something was different . . ." My thoughts faltered and I hesitated trying to regain a verbal handhold on the cliff face within me. Unsure of where I was supposed to belong, I had made the expected effort to blend in, but inwardly I was keenly aware that my life was vastly different from . . . well, different from everyone else's.

Which sounded really dumb.

Of course my life was different from everyone else's.

21

Everyone's life was different from everyone else's.

My thoughts rambled on and on as my words trailed off and mingled with the distant sounds of traffic. I hugged myself, as I sat on the crumbling concrete-block wall, in an effort to keep warm in the crisp, autumn air and stared abjectly at the starry sky above me.

The wind nipped at my St. Cloud State sweatshirt, and although it was a bit nippy for me, I was sure that Jason was comfortable in his T-shirt. I pulled myself away from my thoughts long enough to look over at him, his eyes were fixed on my face and I noticed that they had gone from hazel to a deep shade of green. I sheepishly smiled at him and realized that I probably sounded either incredibly narcissistic or completely idiotic . . . maybe both. He must have felt my embarrassment because he reached for my hand.

He didn't say a word.

He didn't have to.

22

....

Jason and I met in a required, freshman level Speech course.

Room 111 of the Math & Science building at St. Cloud State

University, worlds away from the little girl of six that I had once

been. The red brick building was the largest on campus and had

four large towers containing ominous, concrete stairwells at each

corner of the building. One of my Biology professors frequently

referred to them as missile silos, which was almost believable, given

their shape and size.

On the second day of class, our Speech professor asked us to

write down one interesting thing about ourselves. He compiled the

list and set us loose to connect our classmates with their matching

line of interest.

"Hey, my name is Jason." I heard a voice say nonchalantly.

I looked up from my assignment into a pair of hazel eyes. He thrust

his hand in my direction for a handshake and I reciprocated while

studying him.

"Medium build, lean. Hmm, six feet tall, give or take an inch or two. Charming smile, which wouldn't be so disarming without the boyish overbite. Seems friendly," I thought suspiciously.

"Joyce," I said.

He grinned, "Nice to meet you. Now, you wouldn't happen to be one of the six girls listed on this piece of paper that has their belly button pierced, would you?"

I involuntarily wrinkled my nose and shook my head. "Do I look like the kind of girl who put a belly button piercing down as interesting?" I retorted.

Undeterred by my response, he replied, "Nah, but a guy can hope, can't he?" He winked. "You wouldn't want to make it easy on me and just tell me which one is you?"

"I'm the one who lived in Alaska," I said quietly, as I pointed to the bulleted point below "eighteen tattoos".

"Really? That must have been incredible." He said. He seemed genuinely interested in continuing the conversation, but as I looked around me, everyone else was moving on to the next person.

He kept his gaze steady on me, unaware of the movement around us and I felt intoxicatingly uncomfortable.

"Umm, I think our time is up," I said, averting my eyes. "It-it was nice meeting you," I quickly moved on to the next person, still feeling a little unsettled when I realized I had forgotten to ask which bullet point was his.

As the semester progressed, it seemed like I was forever running into Jason around campus. I saw him at dorm mixers, in the halls, at the cafeteria. I even bumped into him at the coffee cart.

There was no escaping him.

It was a warm Tuesday afternoon, when my dance instructor informed the Modern Dance class that today our lesson would be held outside due to a scheduled repainting of the studio. Rather than cancel class, which I was personally rooting for, my instructor marched to the manicured center of campus and told us to explore the various levels of dance there among the trees, shrubs, and stone sculptures. It was as if, Cirque du Soleil had eaten sixteen women in pink tights and black leotards and vomited the offending mass up onto a college campus.

My face flushed as pink as my tights when I saw him round the corner onto the path towards us. His mouth gaping open, Jason stopped dead in his tracks. He stood there audaciously for what felt like hours and then doubled over in laughter. Catching his breath, he winked at me and headed off in the opposite direction.

The next day in speech class, he leaned over during the lecture and whispered, "That was a pretty hot outfit you had on yesterday." He was close enough that I could smell the clean fragrance of his cologne and I felt his warm breath on the nape of my neck.

I turned in my chair just as he gave me a devilish wink. I made a mental note that he winked an awful lot. Maybe more than anyone I had ever known.

"Thanks, I thought you might like it," I grimaced, trying not to blush again.

Just as I spoke, I heard a forced cough from the front of the classroom. I bit my lip and turned to face the professor who raised an eyebrow in my direction before continuing with his lecture on attentive listening. I heard Jason laughing quietly behind me as the rest of the class resumed taking notes. The desire to crawl under my desk grew with every tick of the second hand as the next twenty minutes dragged on.

"The research portions of your mid-term projects will be due next week. This will comprise fifty percent of your final grade. I am giving you the benefit of a heads up regarding the assignment; however, I will be extremely surprised if you all come prepared," The professor stated boredly.

"His confidence in us is astounding," I thought, still stinging from his non-verbal reprimand.

After class, as we all shuffled out the narrow door into the crowded hallway. I felt a hand on my shoulder and jumped.

"Hey, I didn't mean to startle you. I overheard you discussing your final project with one of the girls this morning in class. If you need a hand on your survey, I have a couple of buddies on my floor that would be willing to help you out, especially if it means a parking ramp closer to the dorms." Jason said.

"It's just a speech for a class, I don't think I'll be getting anyone a parking ramp anytime soon." I said shrugging my bag onto my shoulder. "But - -," I hesitated as I bit my bottom lip. "If you think your friends would be willing to help me out, I wouldn't say no." I added.

"No problem, why don't you come over to Sherburne, 11th floor around eight tonight. Here's my number, if you need it." He said while slipping me a piece of paper with his number on it.

Eight o'clock found me standing in the hallway of the 11th floor of Sherburne Hall next to Jason, with six pairs of eyes trained on me.

"Hey, I'm Big J," said a deep voice.

I looked up at the towering figure before me. "Of course you are," I said laughing.

"If it doesn't work out with Jason, I'm always available," he said scratching the beginnings of a goatee on his chin.

"Uh, thanks - - I think?" I said warily.

"Ignore him," said the next guy in the semi-circle. Big J punched him on the shoulder. I'm Greg, this is my girlfriend Jen."

His right arm was thrown around a brunette's shoulder. She smiled at me sympathetically as Greg lobbed a punch back at Big J with his left fist.

I smiled back.

The rest of the introductions continued.

"Brandon, but you can call me Brando-Bear,"

"Josh."

"Brian."

"Thanks for doing this, it's just five questions to answer," I quickly explained as I handed out the printed slips of paper. Jason and I waited as they filled out their answers and handed them back to me. Once all the slips of paper had been accounted for, one by one the guys excused themselves to head back to their rooms. Some nodding or winking at Jason as they left.

"I think Big J was hitting on me," I said uncertainly, as the two of us were left alone in the hall.

"I'm sure he was," Jason said laughing.

Jason sat down against a wall and I slid down the painted concrete blocks and joined him. We chatted about classes and which professors to avoid. We both grew quiet and I could feel his eyes tracing the profile of my face. My cheeks went warm. I abruptly made an excuse, said goodnight, and made a plan to avoid him for the rest of my life.

But somewhere between my physics class and November, I forgot my silent vow to avoid Jason. "Please don't pick up, please don't pick u---," I murmured to my cell phone as I began to think that I would be able to back out this brain-dead idea.

No such luck, "Hey! - - - - You! It's Joyce from Speech class!" I said a little too high pitched.

Pause.

"Uh-huh, yeah, I was actually heading to the mall."

Pause.

"Yeah, some company would be great."

Pause.

"I'll pick you up in a few minutes." I heard myself say.

I pushed "End Call" and thumped the phone against my forehead, "Stupid, stupid, stupid."

"Thanks for, you know, coming with me." I said an hour later, browsing the sale books on the large wooden shelves.

"No problem. It's a good excuse to get out of my dorm." He replied from the other side of the shelf.

"Can't hack college life?" I glanced up from the row of books and tilted my head back, listening for a comeback to my jab.

"Nah, I just don't have a car here. I sold it so that I wouldn't have the extra payment to worry about while I'm in school, but now that I have you. . ." there was a playfulness to his voice and now it was his turn to wait for a snappy comeback.

"So, you're using me for my car?" I feigned shock as I peered around the shelf that separated us.

"Maybe, I'm using your car as an excuse to see you." He stepped closer and I looked away. My cheeks felt warm.

31

"Uh, do you know what time it is? I'm meeting some friends tonight in Minneapolis." I looked at my shoes not wanting to make eye contact.

"Five fifteen," he said simply after he glanced at his phone.

"Oh. We should probably go. I mean you're more than welcome to come, but I'm going to church tonight." I said suddenly breathless. "Well, sort of." I offered the hurried invitation as we walked out of the bookstore.

"Sure, I've got nothing going on tonight." He said in his familiar go-with-the -flow tone. I felt my stomach do a back-flip.

"Stop it," I thought at my stomach.

"What church?"

We continued walking through the congested mall, weaving between shoppers.

"It's at a club. The New Union. Have you heard of it?" I asked.

He shook his head "No".

I shrugged. "Most of the time they slot bands to play, but on Sunday nights they have a worship service."

32

We walked out of the mall and were welcomed with a blast of cool, autumn air. The crunch of windblown leaves under our feet kept the tempo as we walked towards my blue Toyota.

"So, ummm, what are your beliefs? I mean, seeing as we are going to church together and all, kinda seems like a fair question." I asked.

"I dunno, I guess you could say that I'm taking a break from my faith. I don't see how a loving God could allow hurtful things to happen to people." He shrugged and continued. "My little brother had a couple of brain tumors as a kid. They were benign, but he still had to have two brain surgeries to remove them." He paused as we waited for a black Escalade to pass us. "The first tumor crushed his pituitary gland and stunted his growth. He was a small for his age and the doctors started running tests to find out what was going on." He said casually.

"Sounds intense. How is he now?" I asked as I stepped forward and unlocked the car doors.

"He's fine now, but the tumor affected his sight. He won't ever be able to drive." He said coolly as he sat down in the passenger seat.

"How old is he?" I asked while fiddling with the seat belt.

"Seventeen. Really, I shouldn't call him my "little" brother. He's a beast. He towers over me and I'm 2 years older." He said smiling.

Keys in hand, ready to start the car, I hesitated and turned towards him. I could feel my eyebrows furrowing like a Klingon as I tried to put the pieces together. *"You don't sound all that bitter to me."* I said stating the obvious.

He paused, opened his mouth searching for words and then closed his mouth, kind of like a goldfish blowing water bubbles.

After a few seconds he said, *"You're right, I guess I'm not mad at God."* He paused and then offered, *"Honestly, I guess I just decided to do my own thing. It seemed like a more forgivable excuse to put it all on the back burner because of everything that had happened to my brother. Better to ask forgiveness than permission, right?"*

34

I shook my head at him and he looked like a kid who had just gotten busted with his hand in the cookie jar.

We looked at each other and laughed.

Later that night, electric guitars buzzed through the speakers and the bass reverberated in my chest as we sang "I Could Sing of Your Love Forever".

I had missed this.

I looked around the club and did a double take as I noticed a guy with sleeve tattoos and green mohawk in the far corner. My eyes continued roaming and I scanned down our row. In the dimly lit room I could make out my girlfriends grinning at me, pointing at Jason behind his back and giving me the thumbs up. I mouthed, "stop it" and sent silent daggers through my eyes.

The final notes of the song died out slowly and chairs scuffed against the floor with a metallic ring as we sat down.

Pastor Steve stood up.

"Thanks for coming out tonight. Great worship guys," he said as he turned to the band. He held up his Bible as he turned back

to the rest of us, now seated. "If you brought one, go ahead and open up to Matthew 5. If not, we've got a stack here, go ahead and grab one – it's yours to keep if you need one." He flipped to Matthew 5 and started reading,

"When Jesus saw his ministry drawing huge crowds, he climbed a hillside. Those who were apprenticed to him. The committed, climbed with him. Arriving at a quiet place, he sat down and taught his climbing companions. This is what he said:

> *'You're blessed when you're at the end of your rope. With less of you there is more of God and his rule. You're blessed when you feel you've lost what is most dear to you. Only then can you be embraced by the One most dear to you. You're blessed when you're content with just who you are – no more, no less. That's the moment you find yourselves proud owners of everything that can't be bought.'*

"I'm going to stop right here."

I felt a lump form in my throat.

"Culture today says you've got it made when you've got it all together. When there are no broken pieces of your life to account for. But here, Jesus is saying the opposite. You're blessed when you're at the end of your own strength, your own intelligence, - - your own good looks – Mike, you know I'm talking about you, man. You can't get by on your good looks forever." A chorus of chuckles went up as the guy with the green mohawk stood up and took a bow.

"I'm going to get me some hair like that one day," Pastor Steve said with a chuckle of his own and then continued. "When you find out that you can't save yourself, you're in the best place you could be. Sounds backwards I know, but when you've run out of ideas, determination, and good looks you'll start asking God for help. He's always ready to help you. He wants to help you. But more than that, he wants a relationship with you. He wants to share life with you. Conversations and experiences with you. God is after your heart."

I could feel the tears forming in the corners of my eyes as the feeling of betrayal inched further up my throat. I quickly stuffed it back down.

"Okay, let's go ahead and pray, and if there's anyone here who wants to start that journey with Jesus tonight go ahead and pray this prayer with me. Jesus, I am at the end of my rope. I need You in my life. I need a Savior. I want you in my heart, in the way I think, and in what I do. Thank you, that I am Yours from this day forward. Amen."

A chorus of "Amen's" filled the room and we were released. I hugged my girlfriends, promising to keep in touch.

"What did you think?" I asked glancing over at Jason.

"It was cool. I mean, I've grown up going to church my whole life. I went to a Christian school until high school, so the message wasn't anything new, but it seemed more relevant tonight, you know." His voice grew serious and the silence filled the space between us for a moment. Then he cleared his throat, "Enough about me, what's your story?"

I knew what he was getting at, but my wounds were too fresh and I was still licking most of them.

"What do you mean?" I replied putting on the most naive face I could muster.

"What are your beliefs, you know, where do you stand with God?" he pressed in a voice that mimicked mine from earlier in the day.

I could feel my walls coming up, but I managed a laugh saying, "Jesus is my home-boy."

He kept pressing for more information, "I'm serious."

My mind was racing, this was too soon, and I couldn't deal with this now. I was here to escape all of that.

"Can we not talk about it actually?" My tone grew serious.

He raised one eyebrow and scrutinized me through those now-green eyes.

"What?" I asked defensively.

"Are you sure you don't want to talk about it?" he asked.

I could feel my throat constrict but I wouldn't cry. I couldn't let one more person feel sorry for me.

Anger welled up inside of me and I said forcefully, "No!

Would you just let it drop? I don't want to talk about it."

We rode mostly in silence the rest of the way home.

I felt like such a hypocrite.

I wanted to apologize.

But I couldn't bring myself to say the words.

3

Dirty Filters

God is Mean

I've believed a lot of really wrong things about God.

Mostly in the name of "good" religion.

Things like:

God is loving but he allows horrible things to happen to make us love him back.

Translation: God manipulates to get his way.

And,

God gets all the glory.

Translation: God loves you as long as he gets the credit for saving your sorry self.

And my personal best,

God is holy, so be holy.

Translation: God likes you, *only if,* you follow all of the rules

Of course, no one ever says this stuff out loud.

But everything in my life pointed in one direction.

That direction was marked with road signs that shouted –

GOD IS MEAN.

And no one I knew, really knew God well enough to set the

record straight.

I knew what the Bible said about love and God being love, but

I always read that through the filter of God is harsh and mean

but it all works out in the end.

Sometime after Armageddon.

God was like a drill sergeant in my mind, he got really good

results but didn't care about my feelings or choices. That

filter of my heart where I was supposed to see what love

looked like, was really screwed up.

Stupid filter.

Why isn't there a heart filter company? You know like those pool filter guys who come out and clean the nasty gunk out of pool drains, except for our hearts.

We, and by we, I mean me, need people like that.

I forget sometimes that I actually do have a heart filter guy.

The Holy Spirit is that pool filter guy for my heart. He teaches me right from wrong and why it matters. He holds me and puts me back together when I'm broken. He makes me laugh and lets me cry. And sometimes he does it through other people.

But like I said, the road signs in my life kept screaming that God was just plain mean.

And this has been one of the biggest struggles of life.

Not just mine but all of human kind.

Because this life is a lie.

And that is why it can feel so hard to see who God really is.

This is what we lost in the Garden of Eden.

Our clean heart filters.

It isn't just a kid's Bible story with pictures of a naked couple covered by fig leaves.

It is you.

And it is me.

We bit into the lie that God doesn't care about us.

....

The following Thursday, Jason and I had made plans to meet at McMillan's. The atmosphere was like the food, average with a steady influx of hungry patrons searching for a warm meal. The décor from the late seventies had stagnated over the years as evidenced by its dated wallpaper and Formica tables. Sixty-year old waitresses harboring husky voices chatted the customers up happily. It left much to be desired from an aesthetic view point, but McMillan's made up for it's deficiencies with the obscurity that it befriended us with during the late evening hours. It stayed relatively unpopulated. Usually the back tables were held hostage from 8 – 11 pm by off duty cops. A few scattered tables were occupied by locals and those fortunate enough to stumble across the place.

"I'm sorry about the other night. Let's just say that I've got stuff I need to work through." I paused. "I mean - everyone has stuff, right?" Picking up my fork, I rocked it back and forth across the table. "I think I just need time to sort through some things on my own." I blehed while I continued to fiddle with my fork. I was tense

and I hoped it didn't show. I half expected him to say that he had heard enough. That he thought our friendship, or whatever this was, should end here, but instead he smiled.

"When you're ready to talk, I'm here." He said simply. He made it sound as though he would always be "here".

He changed the subject and we talked late into the night about hobbies (and does anyone still have any?), bad habits, and the random topics that make up conversation. He steered clear of the other night. I could feel my stomach unknot a little.

....

I would have continued; there was so much more to be written, but I had been sitting in the same position for hours. The coveted couch was no longer occupied and I was the only one left in the coffee shop. At two 'o clock in the afternoon, I supposed there wasn't much of a demand for coffee, unless you were an addict.

Which pretty much left just me.

I moved all of my belongings from my ever loyal table to the couch.

"Much better," I thought as I stretched my legs out onto the low lying coffee table in front of me. I rested my laptop on my thighs, pulling my attention back to Jason. I wondered if he would have offered to listen to my story that night if he had known how far its monstrous tendrils would reach. Maybe he felt like one of those eager, young sailors of centuries past, listening to nautical tales of giant squid eating ships and crewmembers. The stories of bravery and excitement feeding into their need for adventure, prompting them to sign aboard the next departing sea-faring vessel only to discover too late that they were fated to become a squid's dinner.

....

Sitting in the campus parking lot after another long night at McMillan's, we sat on the crumbling concrete wall and waited for the campus shuttle to pick us up. It was strange knowing all of the "normalness" that had brought us to this moment on the wall.

48

Nothing in my life had ever been easy or normal. I huddled deeper into my sweatshirt, still holding Jason's hand.

I waited until after we had arrived at my dorm and we were both sitting on my roommate's bed before I unlocked the part of me that kept hammering away in my head, demanding to be let out. My roommate had gone home for the weekend so I pawed at her comforter like a stray cat and found a comfortable spot to nestle down in.

Her poster of Ricky Martin hung directly above her bed and I mindlessly stared at it.

"Is your offer from the other night still good?" I turned towards Jason when I was answered with silence and saw that he was responding with a sympathetic smile and an expression that said, "I'm listening."

I blew a piece of hair out of my eyes, "Well, I guess it would have started with my mother . . ." I began.

My mother.

Kwan-Suk Kim.

49

"Ruth" was her American name.

She was born in South Korea near the village of Pyeongtaek.

She was deaf.

Brown eyes, black hair.

Facts.

All I knew of her were the facts.

But facts don't make a person.

I know the color of her eyes and the color of her hair, but had I ever really known her? I supposed if I closed my eyes, I could imagine her as a child against the backdrop of a country whose land still bears the scars of war. Her trees had all been destroyed, a bitter reminder to the Korean people of the Japanese occupation. However, her landscape still retains some semblance of its former glory. The countryside remains blanketed by rice paddies. Seas of green, during the monsoon seasons. The air is heady with the scents of spices and goods from the open air markets. There is a melding of past and present and a tangible hope for a bright future among the people. This is plainly seen in the cities, where open air markets co-exist with skyscrapers and billboards, and older women carry plastic bags of groceries on their heads alongside the Korean business man who hurries along with his briefcase in hand. Older men can be seen playing Mah Jong on a table outside a storefront while soldiers from the nearby U.S. Army base stand by to watch how the game will unfold. The old values are still cherished while allowing for the advancement of their culture.

And yet, for all of its wonder and complexity, South Korea, like any country, has its faults as well. There is little room for mistakes or abnormalities, even her people are judged according to their flaws. Orphanages can be found in numbers in South Korea. The deaf, the blind, and the "unfit" for society can be found here. As children they are often abandoned at the orphanages, and most will spend their entire lives there.

51

This was my mother's story. Abused and abandoned at an orphanage. She ran away looking for the family that had left her but she was never able to find them. Instead, she found herself in the red light district. After months of scraping by on what she could earn and finding it not enough, she eventually returned to the orphanage and there she stayed.

I've seen a few worn, old photographs from her life as an adult in the orphanage. She stayed there because she had nowhere to go. She looks complacent, but not happy. She is smiling, but her eyes seem far away. Sadness. Loneliness, perhaps. She had black hair that fell past her shoulders, brown eyes, and childlike hands.

I held up my hands like a mime in a bank heist, "I have my mother's hands," I said simply. I think what I meant to say was, "I went through my messed up childhood and all I have to show for it are these little hands. Talk about your lame souvenirs."

I paused and glanced at Jason, wondering if I should continue or if he had fallen asleep listening to me go on about my mother. He was stretched out on the floor, propped up on his right side and cradling the right side of his head in his hand.

He was awake. Score for the itty, bitty hand girl!

"Did your mother tell you much about her childhood?" he asked gently.

"You know, I can't remember a single conversation about her childhood," I confessed. "Most of what I know, I've gathered in monosyllabic conversations over the years from my dad. He doesn't really talk about her." I shook my head and shrugged my shoulders. "It was really rough on my dad . . ." I stopped when I saw Jason's face wrinkle into a quizzical look and knew I was getting ahead of myself. "Sorry, I'm jumping ahead," I apologized, squinching my left eye closed and pinching my lips together with my fore-fingers. "Do you actually want to listen to my sob story some more?" I asked skeptical, glancing at the Pepto-pink alarm clock near my roommate's bed. Twelve o' clock.

"No, I want you to keep going. But under one condition. I'm starving; let's order some pizza or something." He said without looking up at the clock.

Still perched on top of the bed with my legs crossed in front of me, I glanced down at him. "Seriously? We just ate four hours ago." I said, raising an eyebrow.

He had a mischievous gleam in his eye as he reached up to the bed. Suddenly he grabbed a pillow and threw it at me. "Don't you know that the way to a guy's heart is through his stomach? How do you ever plan on keeping me if you won't feed me?"

I laughed.

Six pieces of pizza, four breadsticks, and a can of Sprite later; Jason was finally full. I think.

He interrupted my thoughts, "I think you left off at your dad."

"Right."

My dad.

"My dad doesn't speak much of his own childhood. When he was eighteen, he enlisted in the Army. His first assignment overseas was to South Korea, and he was stationed at an Army base in Pyeongtaek called Camp Humphreys." I rattled the information off like I was reading a Wikipedia entry.

"So you're an Army brat, huh?" Jason sat up and repositioned his back against the bed.

I saluted to confirm, while I took a sip from a can of Sprite.

"I actually don't know the full story about how my parents met. He doesn't really talk about my mother if he can help it. I only know he met her at the orphanage he volunteered at." I said. "She taught my dad sign language while he was helping out at the orphanage."

"Wait, your dad had to learn sign language to communicate with her?" Jason asked in disbelief.

"Yeah, I guess you could say it was the ultimate romantic gesture." I could feel a wry smile spread across my face.

"Have you asked your dad about it? You know, really sat down and had a father to daughter chat?" Jason asked.

55

I tucked my hair behind my ear, "You don't know my dad. Don't get me wrong, he's a great guy, he'd give you the shirt off his back, but he's very much the quiet, military type. Besides, I think he's been through enough." I commented like a sportscaster on ESPN. Smooth, cool, and onto the next highlight.

"Hey, this is me listening again and not asking probing questions," Jason said, catching the drift.

I nodded, not meeting his eyes.

We sat in silence for a few moments.

"So they got married," he stated.

"Yeah and then my dad was reassigned by Uncle Sam to Ft. Campbell, Kentucky. She got her green card and followed. They became pregnant with me a year later. A year or two after I was born, my dad was reassigned to Alaska for four years." I said frowning at my roommate's bedspread. I folded creases into the bedspread and smoothed them out again.

I sighed. "It was when we moved to Alaska that my mother became schizophrenic, or the symptoms began to show, or - -I-- I don't know." I tried to explain. I sighed again and bit the right

56

corner of my bottom lip. I always hated telling people this part.

One, because I hated reliving it and two, because it felt so surreal to

tell it. This stuff didn't happen in life – not real life anyways.

Maybe, that was how my father felt. And why he never

talked about it. But it felt dishonest to who I was to always keep it

bottled up. So when I was younger, I tried to tell a few people who I

thought wouldn't feel sorry for me . . . but after the fifth or sixth time

I couldn't stomach the sad smiles and eyes laced with pity.

Eventually, I became just as mum about the whole ordeal as my dad.

I hated being pitied.

No, worse, I despised it.

It made me feel as though, because life had dealt me a raw

blow, I was some weird anomaly, like Gonzo on the Muppets. On

the other hand, there were those people who looked at me in awe for

surviving, as if I had parted the Red Sea or something. And that

was equally as embarrassing. I didn't want to be Gonzo or Moses.

I just wanted to be me.

"I know some people accept schizophrenia as some sort of

mental illness that just is, and I guess I don't have anything else to compare it to, but the things that used to happen in my house were . .

. ummm . . . evil." I grew quiet. I swallowed. "My mother would do

things that could rival characters in a Stephen King novel." I said

quietly.

I knew what was said about my mother, despite the discrete

whispers. I remembered the nights spent with different families from

church while "issues" at home were sorted out.

I don't remember having friends over to our house at all.

Ever.

....

I returned from my conversation with Jason and was

instantly brought back to my present; my cozy coffee shop. I stopped

typing and stared at my hands.

My mother's hands.

The same hands from the orphanage pictures.

....

"My mother," I took a moment to clear my throat, *"believed that I was conceived by Immaculate Conception. My dad was stunned, you know, since he was there for the making of little 'ol me."* I reached for my Sprite. *"She would have these episodes where she would rage at my dad, saying that Jesus couldn't save her, that he wasn't the Son of God; he was Buddha's brother."* I recounted tracing the rim of my can. Jason didn't say anything.

"So, wouldn't that make Buddha my uncle then? You know, according to her, if I was conceived by Immaculate Conception and he was Jesus' brother?" I half smiled at my weak attempt at a joke. Jason didn't laugh.

"Come on, that was a little funny," I said flashing a full smile.

He gave me a lop-sided grin but it didn't touch his eyes.

"Here comes the pity," I thought, gritting my teeth. I kept talking hoping that if I just muscled through it that I would never have to talk about it after tonight.

"I used to sleep with my parents as a baby and I guess there was this one night . . . my dad heard a noise from my mother's side of the bed. When he looked for me, he saw that she was trying to suffocate me," I swallowed hard. *"Her defense was that she was trying to spare me from a painfully difficult childhood . . . she didn't want to see me suffer as she had,"* I shrugged as I bit my thumbnail, *"I stopped sleeping with my parents."* I glanced at Jason and continued, recounting my past as if it were just a collection of facts gathered from a newspaper. I didn't want to feel my way through it. I just wanted to tell him and be done with it. I continued reciting as best as I could remember.

"My dad also stopped sleeping with my mother. I mean, I think he just stopped sleeping," I set my can down on the floor and absent-mindedly chewed on my thumbnail, nervous for what Jason's reaction would be once my sorry little tale had been told. *"He would lay awake night after night, bracing for her hallucinations,"* I took a deep breath. *"Her arms and legs would flail uncontrollably."* I murmured, hoping my simple explanations were enough. *"She would scream and thrash around, punching and kicking at unseen*

demons. 'They were coming for her,' she said. She could see them. She could see their eyes as they were coming to rape her."

I stared at the floor, but I was far away. After a few moments, the tangible silence tapped me on the shoulder with its invisible presence and brought me back to my dorm room with Jason.

I didn't look at him. I just kept talking, afraid that if I stopped I would never find the courage to start again. "My dad sent me to stay with friends from our church, while my mother went through treatment and then, I don't know - everything seemed to be in remission." I suddenly felt cold. "And –," I could feel the ache throbbing in my chest. "- and then one day, my dad came home from work to see a four- year old me sitting at the bottom of the stairs. 'Mommy's acting funny,' I told him. He went upstairs to find my mother screaming at him. He found her mid-hallucination, flailing. She signed that he looked like a demon, a monster coming to get her. She lunged at him, trying to claw his eyes out with her fingernails."

I grew quiet, straining to forget.

"How does a deaf woman scream?" Jason haltingly asked.

*I blinked and met his eyes, grateful for the change in subject,
"They can still make noises with their vocal cords." A small laugh
escaped from between my lips, "It's kinda crazy, but deaf people can
be louder than hearing people."*

*Talking about my mother always made me feel vulnerable
and I swore I would never be that way again, but somehow talking
about it tonight made all of my repressed emotions bubble up to the
surface. I wished they would just bubble away like the carbonation
in my Sprite can.*

"I do have a few good memories of her," I said softly.

"Tell me," he urged.

*"We used to play cards. I remember it was late at night and
the house was dark except for the dining room light above the kitchen
table. We all took turns thumping the table when there was an
UNO."*

"Tell me another one," Jason said.

*"I have this memory of the two of us sitting on the kitchen
floor making kimchee." I paused. "You know what "kimchee" is,
right?" I asked Jason.*

He smirked at me and replied, "Yeah, it's that horrible smelling cabbage that you, Koreans eat."

"Hey, have you ever tried it? It's kinda like the sauerkraut you, Germans, eat, just spicier . . . and better tasting." I fired back as I crossed my arms, laughing.

"So, why did you sit on the floor to make it?" Jason asked.

I shrugged, "Tradition?"

The funny thing was that there wasn't an extraordinary bonding moment that took place as we sat on the floor making kimchee. I think I remember it simply because it was one of the only peaceful memories of my mother and me.

I frowned as another memory took shape.

Jason must have sensed my hesitation, because he touched my knee and said, "When you're ready."

Grateful, I nodded my head and glanced at the alarm clock. 2:47 AM. We both stood and I followed him to the door.

"Goodnight," I said leaning against the open doorframe.

"'Night," he yawned.

SCATTERED

I closed the door behind him. I was spent, but instead of crawling into bed I pulled up a stool and gingerly fingered the dusty keys on my keyboard. I hadn't played since I started classes this past fall. I hesitated for a moment and noticed my hands.

My mother's hands.

My hands.

I played for an hour, willing the pain out of my heart and into the music.

4

Night Vision Goggles

Seeing in the Dark

It was densely black out that night.

Like coffee with no creamer.

As a thirteen year old, I should have been home, tucked into my bed.

But as an Army brat, I had a reputation to uphold for pushing boundaries . . . and my dad's buttons.

I was out way past curfew.

My dad thinking I was staying at a friend's house for the night.

Just like I said I was.

But the stars winked at me, promising to keep my secret, and my friends and I spent the night in a farmer's field on the edge of the city.

Let me be the first to tell you, this was not the brightest idea we had ever had.

Around midnight, there was a rustle behind us.

Suddenly, we were surrounded by a unit of soldiers running nighttime drills.

See, I told you.

Definitely not a bright idea.

One of us screamed like a girl.

I'm almost positive it was one of the boys.

Another one let out a string of something unintelligible.

But it was my friend, Jim who pulled a Forrest Gump and made it home before anyone could tell him there wasn't any real danger.

The G.I. Joes with their faces painted in grease paint, howled with laughter.

One of them even tried to call after Jim, telling him it was okay.

But Jim never did find the guts to come back that night.

The rest of us stayed and hung out with the commandos in camo.

We asked about their night vision goggles and they let us take turns looking through them.

When it was my turn, I squinted into the darkness that settled over the field in front of me.

It was hard to see more than a few feet.

I moved the night vision goggles up to my eyes.

I could see everything like it was day.

Okay, so it was more like a lime green kind of day.

But everything was clear.

The rows of planted rice.

The far tree line.

More soldiers moving through the trees just beyond the field.

I could make out things in the darkness that I hadn't been able
to see before.

Sweet clarity.

That was what I wanted more than anything from my writing
when I first started.

For things in my life to make sense.

To be clear.

Because all I could see behind me and on the long road ahead,
was that everyone, including God - had left me.

Left Behind.

It wasn't just a book series . . . it could have been tattooed across my forehead.

Which is maybe true for more than just me.

We have been squinting into the darkness of our lives, not able to make out the figures in the distance.

Believing that we are alone.

But writing is a lot like using night vision goggles.

It helps us to see past the darkness.
It helps us to find that we aren't as alone as we once believed.

....

Seemingly overnight, it was as if celestial dump trucks converged on our campus. Old man winter had personally ensured that the conspiracy was executed flawlessly. Make-shift sleds from cafeteria trays soon appeared and those courageous enough to venture outdoors were taken hostage by the winter wonderland.

The rest of us, too frozen to think of anything besides microwaved mugs of hot cocoa and instant coffee, kept our wits about us and were able to resist the winter madness plaguing the rest of the student body. We stayed indoors, buried in piles of exams and papers.

Jason and I sat huddled together under a blanket in the student lounge. It was a typically quiet - albeit lazy, Saturday afternoon. I moved my head to his lap and studied the overgrowth of brown whiskers on his chin. He hadn't shaved for the last couple of days.

I wasn't sure if I could love a lumberjack.

My thoughts snapped back like a stretched rubber band, as I heard him mention my mother. "Ready to talk about your mother

71

again?" he stated abruptly. I didn't say anything and just stared at the water stains on the ceiling. They were fascinating. They didn't ask me questions about overdue papers or final exams or mentally ill mothers.

Life should be more like a water stain.

Jason's eyebrows furrowed together as he thought, and after a few seconds said, "You were living in Alaska and she attacked your dad."

"Are you sure you're not majoring in psychology?" I glared at him.

He raised his eyebrows and smiled slyly, "Maybe I should."

I rolled my eyes and blew out a short breath.

My mind raced backwards in time as I relived my personal hell.

I was six. My mommy was sick. She was on lots of medications to make her feel better and sometimes she stayed overnight at the hospital until she felt good enough to come home.

Sometimes she would stay for months. Dad was worried, but he didn't talk much about it and I didn't ask questions.

The Army reassigned my dad to Ft. Rucker, Alabama. After moving south, life settled into a natural rhythm for us. We moved into a brick, quad-style, apartment in the city of Enterprise. We got a dog. A miniature Shetland sheepdog named Tippy. He looked like a little Lassie. No white picket fence since we lived in an apartment, but a dog, that was something normal families had right?

We found a new church and I started at school. I began to make friends. My best friend was a boy who lived next door to us in our apartment building. We would go exploring through the wooded areas around our house, spending countless hours playing in the sandbox, or just running around in the backyard playing games. Stuff normal kids do.

My mother seemed to be doing better for a while and the psychiatrists told my dad that I would be safe to stay at home with her. But I always wondered who was watching who?

Was I supposed to watch her and keep her safe?

73

What kind of abnormal behavior was I looking for?

And if I was taking care of her, then who was taking care of me?

"She had a couple of friends who were deaf and she would go to their houses while my dad was at work. Their conversations were usually about how unhappy she was. I didn't really want to go. I didn't want to be there, not with them, and not with her. I remember trying to distract myself by doing other things so that I didn't have to see the words that she was signing."

I sighed and looked up at Jason.

Why was this so hard to talk about?

But Jason just gave me an encouraging look and so I kept rambling on.

"But then, I dunno, things went from sort of normal to bad. Her hallucinations started again. Books, especially the Bible, never seemed to stay on the shelves for long. They were the first things to be thrown. The things she saw sent her blindly flying to the walls, grappling for something, anything to use as weapons or shields. She

went back to the hospital more frequently. I secretly hoped she would stay forever, because I was so afraid of her." I stopped and looked up at my comforting water stain on the ceiling.

"I had made a get-well-soon card for my mother after one of her hospitalizations. I had drawn a picture of us, as a family, on the front. On the inside of the card, I had written that if she just tried harder she could get better. My dad saw the card before I had the chance to give it to her." I grew somber remembering the conversation that followed.

"Why does she have to be so selfish? If she tried she could get better for us," I bitterly told my dad.

My dad ran a hand through his quickly graying hair and tactfully pointed out that I should make a different card.

I bit the inside of my cheek and came back to my conversation with Jason, "I threw my card away and when my mother came home, I had nothing to give her."

The move hadn't helped her to get better - it felt like things just kept getting worse. My dad got a phone call at work one day

75

from the police saying that a woman meeting his wife's description was found standing in the middle of the highway. She had stepped out in front of a semi-truck. She was suicidal again. Her medications would need to be reevaluated and she would need to go back to the hospital. He left work early that day to go and get her from the police station.

"It never changed. She would improve, come home from the hospital, and then attempt to kill herself - - or one of us and inevitably . . . be readmitted." I rubbed my eyes hoping it would clear my head and a sardonic laugh slipped out.

"Lather, Rinse, Repeat." I said, more to my water stain than to Jason.

It was a cycle that never ended. My dad tried to shelter me from it as much as possible. He arranged for friends to baby sit me as often as he could. He rarely spoke about my mother, maybe hoping I didn't know what was happening.

But I knew.

My mother spent months at a time in psych hospitals, undergoing drug treatments and therapy sessions. She once confessed to a therapist that she had taken one of my dad's hunting rifles while we lived in Alaska and had held it to the back of his head while he watched TV.

He never knew.

She continued to tell the therapist that she would have pulled the trigger but a voice told her, "If you kill him, they will take Joyce away from you." I never knew where that tiny voice of reason came from that kept my mother from pulling the trigger that day; I'd like to think God sent an angel to whisper in her ear.

As the years progressed, my mother's condition intensified, and she moved once again from the realm of fantasizing about suicide to acting it out. And then my mother began making threats again to her therapists and to my dad that she was going to kill me.

My dad did the only thing he could think of to protect me. He asked several friends of his from church to watch me. Again, as before, I began living at other people's houses. It wasn't funded by the Department of Human Services and managed by social workers, but it was still foster-care.

In Alaska, I had gone to other people's houses after school,
and now, here I was in Alabama doing it all over again. Friends of
my dad's, from church, would pick me up from school and I would
often fall asleep on their couches waiting for my dad to come and get
me after work. Usually he came around 9 pm or so, but sometimes
later, depending on work or my mother. I would often be carried out
to his truck, half asleep. I still remember the coarse, scratchy
material of his military fatigues on my cheek and the oddly
comforting smell of helicopter fuel mingled with boot polish.

My dad repeatedly felt the jarring loss of holding onto my
mother. He sacrificed much, hoping and praying that God would
heal her. He lost friends, family, money and even his truck. I
suppose his truck in many ways was a grown man's equivalent to my
stuffed raccoon. Less cuddly, but still the one thing that he had to
himself. He sold it to cover her medical expenses.

And then one day things just went black.

A friend of my dad's had picked me up after school that day. I wasn't safe at home anymore. In fact, I lived with other people more often than with my own family. I didn't even know what a home was supposed to be. And after sleeping on countless couches and pretending that I was fine, I didn't care anymore. I didn't feel anymore.

My dad came home from work to find my mother passed out on the kitchen floor. He found an empty Symmetrel bottle, a medication used to treat Parkinson's disease and on occasion, schizophrenia. It wasn't recommended for patients who had suicidal tendencies.

My father called 911. The EMTs transported her to the hospital where her stomach could be pumped. She had taken 30 pills. Five pills at her dosage could kill a person easily. She would code three times in the ambulance on the way to the hospital. The EMTs were able to revive her each time, but barely.

My father was told by the medical staff that had he come home 20 minutes later, she would have been dead.

I'll always wonder if a small part of him wished he would have come home later. Wished that in the space of 20 minutes, he could have a normal life back.

A chance to start over.

A chance to rebuild his family.

A chance to sleep through the night without the fear that the woman lying next to him in bed would destroy everything he had once hoped for.

I remember hating my mother when I found out what she had done. After all that my dad had done, after all we had sacrificed, how could she be so selfish?

She came home and life returned to the pattern that I knew was unique to our family. I still lived in constant fear of my mother, but I refused to let it show. Instead I was defiant, yet always aware that she could kill me if given the chance. Was there any part of my mother that was still in that shell?

Life didn't stay "normal" for long. My dad received another call at work from the police saying that his wife had stood in the middle of a busy intersection and attempted to jump in front of

traffic, again.

I learned from personal experience that history does in fact

repeat itself.

He went to the police station.

She went back to the hospital.

And I went to sleep at the neighbor's house.

....

There's a picture of me as a bright-eyed kid in a rainbow

stripped t-shirt sitting on the floor with my back propped up against

our blue patterned couch, legs straight out and crossed at the ankles.

I have my right hand submerged in a cereal box with our dog,

Tippy, sitting to my left waiting for a few sugary morsels to fall to

unclaimed territory.

I look happy.

81

This was how I remembered Saturday mornings with my dad, when my mother was gone in the hospital. We would sit together on the floor, backs propped up by the couch. We'd sit munching on dry cereal, legs crossed at the ankles with the dog hoovering fallen bits of cereal. My dad was different when my mother was gone.

Relaxed.

He would polish his black military boots with the tin of polish that had the kiwi bird on it. I'll never forget the pungent odor of the black polish wafting through the house. The quintessential military smell. It reminded me of helicopters and camouflaged uniforms.

He would do normal things like laundry, brush the dog, and watch TV. Sometimes, before he would leave for his field exercises he would reorganize and repack his standard issue, military green duffle bag. If I was lucky, he would give me his leftover MRE's when he got back from the field. I took all of the dehydrated peaches. We would spend the mornings putzing around the house and in the afternoons we would go catch a movie at the theater, followed by dinner at a restaurant.

Sundays were reserved for church. Afterwards, we would go out to eat. My dad would usually nap on Sunday afternoons and I would play videogames. Then Monday would come and for my dad it was off to work and for me it was off to school and my other life, where my mother was nothing more than a bad dream.

And yet, she was always with me, in my thoughts, my emotions, my very being. She was as close to me as the marrow in my bones. She was the reason for every jarring change that yanked me from my current reality to the next.

When Tippy died, my dad got a new dog and we named her Princess. She too, was a Shetland sheepdog – a mini-Lassie. My dad was brushing her one day to remove the sandburs that had gotten caught in her long fur, when she began to whine and jerk away suddenly. She cried frantically and shied away from being touched. After he had gotten her to calm down, he began to look through her fur and saw a deep, long burn that ran the length of her back. He brought her into the vet who after examining her determined that she had been burned by a hot liquid. It resulted in a 3rd degree burn and Princess avoided my mother after that.

My mother never confessed, but my dad suspected that she had poured a hot liquid down her back. The scar looked too straight to be an accident. The vet shaved Princess' fur and treated the burn, but Princess carried a 2 inch by 12 inch scar down her back for the rest of her life.

After several incidents, my mother was around less than ever. She was committed to a mental health facility an hour away from our apartment.

I rarely, if ever saw her.

My dad faithfully visited her and took care of her, but he never brought me with to see her. And I never asked to go. I often wondered at his unfailing dedication to her. When other marriages had dissolved under much less pressure, he remained steadfast.

Was it hope that bound him to her?

A sense of moral obligation?

Or after all that he had suffered and all that he had silently borne, did he still love her?

There was political unrest in the Middle East and my dad was working 12 -14 hour days as a helicopter mechanic for the Army. I continued to stay with other families after school, but soon it wasn't enough. The Gulf War broke out and my dad's hours increased. He began to ask friends of his at our church if a more permanent living situation could be arranged with them for me until things settled down with the war.

My mother had long since been dead to me and now my dad was gone, the Army laying claim to his time.

I had gone from foster-care to an orphan.

....

My journaling file on my thumb drive was now bursting at the seams and my brain kinda felt the same way too. So I closed my laptop, eager to return when there was a free moment to steal away.

I smiled.

Writing was helping.

The emotional clutter that had been collecting in mountainous piles in my heart was slowly being sorted through. Some things were kept, others thrown away but everything was being put in its place. And somehow, that knowledge gave me hope. If things were starting to make sense now that I was putting my life down on paper then God definitely could make sense of the life behind the words.

"You know, God, this would have been a lot easier if I would have started writing when I was a kid." I pictured little Asian me, emerging from the womb armed with a pint-sized laptop, pushing my oversized glasses up onto my nose.

"But hey, I would have missed reaping the benefits of sipping coffee chock full of antioxidants, caffeine, and sugar. Not to mention, developing my now, blossoming talent for cynicism." I thought sarcastically as I cradled my chin in my right palm.

I rolled my eyes at myself and blew a stray piece of hair out of my line of sight, cringing inwardly at life's twisted sense of humor. I had to live it to write it, and now I had to write it to

really learn to live.

Irony.

I could learn to live without it.

....

Jason continued listening, so I just kept talking, "When my

dad wasn't home during the day, my mother would watch movies.

She would try to have me watch them with her when I was home

from school. They were awful. She always wanted to watch really

morbid movies about sacrificial murders and mutilations. I hated it

and one day I hid one of the movies from her. She was furious when

I wouldn't tell her where it had gone. I was scared of her and what

she would do to me. I ran and hid in our laundry closet." I closed

my eyes.

I don't remember how long I stayed in the closet staring at

the wood-grained, shuttered closet doors. It was dark and only

dimly lit by the rays of light coming through the door. I could see occasional movement if I peered between the wood slats, but she never found me. I don't remember how long I stayed in the laundry closet, it may have been minutes or hours, but it felt like days passed before I came out.

I took a deep breath and continued with my eyes still closed, "When my dad came home, I told him what she had been doing while he was gone during the day. I showed him where I hid the movie. My parents argued, my dad won, and my mother went back to the hospital." I opened my eyes, my stomach hurt. I didn't want to talk anymore. . . .

"You alright?" Jason asked.

"Yeah, you know. . ." my voice trailing.

My neck was starting to feel stiff so I sat up and leaned against the arm of the couch, crossed my legs and paused. He followed suite and propped himself up against the opposite arm.

"You sure you still want to be friends with a girl like me? It's likely that I have too much baggage for you to deal with." I leaned in and asked playfully, desperate to chase away the shadows of my mother.

"*You're right, I should probably leave now while I still can.*"
He said standing up from the couch.

*Seriously? But then again, I guess I didn't really blame him.
Would I want to be with someone like me?*

"*For the record,*" he calmly continued breaking into my
stunned silence, "*I'm hoping that you consider yourself, your
baggage, and me more than just friends.*" *And with that he kissed
me on the forehead and walked out the door.*

*I continued to sit there in the same position for a solid three
minutes, perplexed by what had happened.* "*What **had** just
happened?*" *And just as I was rehashing the previous conversation,
word for word in my mind, he reappeared smiling.*

"*What was that about?*" *I said shaking my head bewildered.*

"*You didn't think I'd actually leave you hanging like that
did you?*" *he asked winking and I watched as he bent over and
pulled two cans of Pepsi from the pockets on the legs of his tan cargo
pants. He set them on the thinly carpeted floor and stood facing me.*

"I . . . I . . ." I stammered. After stumbling around, my tongue decided to join the rest of my working faculties and I finished, "Seriously?" I said standing and giving his chest a mock push.

He covered my hands with his own over his chest, "I was serious about wanting to be more than friends," as an afterthought he added soberly, "your baggage is still welcome to come along for the ride too."

I glanced downward at my hands still resting on his chest.

Un-com-for-ta-ble.

I was so uncomfortable.

This was the stuff that I had never been good at. And not just in the romantic sense. I was so awkward when it came any emotions between people. Love, loyalty, devotion. Completely foreign to me. But I was torn, I was twisted by a lifetime of skewed perception. Trapped beneath the mangled wreckage of years gone by. I was so confused. Me, damaged beyond repair, unfit for any relationship.

I pulled away, "You don't want to be with someone like me. I'm so damaged." I said.

He led me back towards the couch and held me, the way a father holds a child. He pulled me onto his lap and with my head cradled against his neck, he said simply, "You are," but he kissed me anyways. I could feel the heat radiating from his chest.

His clarity astounded me. He may not have understood my childhood, but he understood me. I gave in. I couldn't remember a time when I had ever been held like this. I nuzzled my head deeper into his neck, like I had done once before with a stuffed raccoon. I breathed him in. The scent of his skin and cologne had now become so familiar and comforting to me.

I breathed him in and I felt safe.

5

Godzilla

God Speaks

God speaks.

All the time.

The problem is, we don't know what he sounds like.

We're waiting for God to show up like Godzilla.

To come stomping across the screens of our lives, crushing everything that plagues us, lower a huge head full of gaping teeth, smile at us and say, "Tah Dah! I'm here to squash your problems."

Not that Godzilla did that . . . okay, fine, bad analogy, but you totally caught my drift, right?

We're missing God because we are looking for the huge, epic moments.

And it is really easy to miss God or get mad at him if you don't know what to listen for.

Sometimes, he does the big moments.

But more often than not, he does the small ones.

Because relationships are built on a million, small moments, spent together.

Then he was told, "Go, stand on the mountain at attention before GOD. GOD will pass by." A hurricane wind ripped through the mountains and shattered the rocks before GOD, but GOD wasn't to be found in the wind; after the wind an earthquake, but GOD wasn't in the earthquake; and after the earthquake fire, but GOD wasn't in the fire; and after the fire a gentle and quiet whisper. When Elijah heard the quiet voice, he muffled his face with his great cloak, went to the mouth of the cave, and stood there. A quiet voice asked, "So Elijah, now tell me, what are you doing here?"

1 Kings 19:11-13
(The Message)

I like the part where it says, "a quiet voice asked."

God asked Elijah what he was doing.

Not because God didn't know.

Not because Elijah was in trouble.

But because as much as we crave to hear the voice of God, he

equally wants to hear us speak back.

It's taken me a long time to realize that God doesn't often

come in like a giant Japanese lizard . . . he usually comes with

a whisper.

He whispers to our hearts.

Somehow, writing helped me to move past the Godzilla

expectation I had of God.

I began to hear him speaking.

And I remember finding the courage to speak back.

I knew he wanted me to work through my childhood.

But life had stomped through me leaving a trail of emotional destruction and I just needed time to be a "normal" human being.

Whatever that was.

So I asked him for time to be "normal".

And the amazing thing?

He heard me.

....

"Ok, favorite Christmas memory as a kid," Jason posed his question more as a statement than a request.

We lay under his parent's Christmas tree staring up at the oversized bulbs and homemade ornaments from Christmas' past in the Ackermann household. I found myself envying Jason's 'perfect' childhood.

"Mmmm, I love Christmas, but I don't have any memories of it as a kid." I spoke into the synthetic pine needles, staring contentedly at the brilliantly colored Christmas lights.

"Really?" he turned his attention from the tree to my face.

"Actually, I don't remember ever having a Christmas tree in our house while my mother was around." I murmured. I took a deep breath, releasing it slowly as I repositioned myself for a new perspective of the tree. "I have to admit, I'm slightly jealous. You have these great family memories and absolutely awful looking reindeer ornaments . . . . Wait, are those made out of clothespins? . .

. to remember Christmas' past by." I mocked. "Oh no, I think this one got run over by a rogue sleigh," I said wrinkling my nose.

"Careful, they can hear you. Besides, I was in kindergarten when I made those," Jason said protectively.

"I think they're great. Really. I love that each ornament has a memory tied to it." I said, now sincere. "I bet your mom was the type to take lots of baby pictures."

"Yeah, she was. She has a box of 'Jason nostalgia' for me when I move out." Jason moved his hands behind his head as he resumed his Christmas tree gazing.

"'Jason nostalgia' huh? What's that?" I asked.

"My old baby blanket, a scrapbook she made for me, my favorite books as a kid, stuff like that," he said.

"Stuff you'll never use again, but it's nice to know she cared?" I asked trying to understand.

"Yeah," he grinned.

"Must be nice," I found myself wistfully thinking.

Within a few months of starting a new job at a home for people with special needs, my life settled. Spring semester ended, Jason moved back in with his parents and I moved into my first apartment with my friend, Allie.

I had finally created a "normal" life for myself. I had a decent apartment, a good job, a great boyfriend, but mostly my life was stable. No seismic shifts in the tectonic plates of my life. I was immensely grateful and I was actually starting to relax a little. The tightness that I had always carried in my stomach from constantly being on guard seemed to unknot itself.

It was a "normal", albeit rainy, Friday night and Jason and I were at the Ackermann house. We had sprawled out on the basement floor in his parent's basement to watch a movie. As the credits scrolled upward, Jason asked "So, what other skeletons do you have in your closet?"

"Ha, wouldn't you like to know!" I dodged.

Bob and weave, Joyce. Bob and weave. I strategized to myself.

"Nah, I wanna know," he countered. I was cornered like some poor wildebeest about to be pounced upon by a ravenously hungry lion. There was no way for me to bow out gracefully, and as far as I could see, no tall, African grasses, ideal for hiding in, existed in the Ackermann basement.

"Hmmm, well I stayed with a Catholic family, moved to Germany, and lived with family that had a dog named Bear . . . that's the CliffNotes version." I said shrugging quickly.

"Catholics, and Germans, and Bear – oh my!" Jason said mimicking the Wizard of Oz.

"Nice," I said laughing. "Okay, so the Wagners were the first family that I officially moved in with. They were Catholic, raised by nuns I think. They had 3 kids. Milly, Nolan, and Caitlin. They saw me as a kid who desperately needed discipline and a stable environment. . ." I laughed and added after a second thought, "They were probably right."

"Their kids were the model of perfect behavior. Me, not so much. I had kind of grown up raising myself in a lot of ways and I

wasn't used to having parents tell me what to do. Plus, I was stubborn."

"I could see that." Jason said unflinchingly.

"Be nice!" I pushed his shoulder. He flashed a mischievous grin.

"I dunno, it could have been worse. I had a roof over my head and food in my stomach." I said thoughtfully. "I didn't stay with the Wagners very long, maybe six months." I chewed on my thumbnail.

"Why?" he asked.

"Ah, well, in the end, they told my dad, in not so many words, that I was having a negative effect on their family and that I couldn't stay with them anymore." I said somberly.

"So, how does Germany fit in?" he interjected.

"After the Wagners, I stayed with other people in our church who offered to keep me for a weekend or a night." A familiar lump started to form in my throat so I hurriedly continued. "And then things began to heat up with the Gulf War and my dad was an Army helicopter mechanic. Mostly Chinooks and Apaches. He

worked 18 hour days as stateside support for Operation Desert

Shield." I recited. "I needed a place to stay and a family from church

took me in."

"Where was your mother?" he asked.

"She was in a mental hospital in Florida."

"Oh," Jason said thoughtfully. "And Germany fits in how?"

"So the family I moved in with was an Air Force family

and they had 4 kids, Burt, Rachel, Bradley, and Becky. I stayed with

them during the week and on the weekends I lived with my dad.

Life was really good with the Halberts. It was normal. I remember

little things about living with them, like singing really loudly to

WilsonPhillips in the car and eating mac and cheese for dinner, and

playing outside in the yard. Normal kid stuff.

"WilsonPhillips, huh?" Jason raised an eyebrow.

"Don't judge, they were very cool back then." I scowled.

"Riiiight, so what? You followed WilsonPhillips to

Germany for their world tour?" he snickered.

"Yes, as an 8-year old back-up singer." I bantered back.

"Okay, no seriously," he said.

"The Halberts were reassigned to Germany for two years. I didn't have anywhere else to go and my dad was out of options. He signed over custody so that I could go with them." I paused. "And they had a black Chow-Chow named Bear." I added.

Catholics, and Germans, and Bear, oh my!" Jason said laughing.

....

"What's wrong with me?" I said out loud to the roof of my car as I pulled into the parking lot of my apartment complex. I pounded the back of my head into the headrest a couple of times for good measure, and then parked my car. How was it that I had gone from maintaining these unscalable emotional walls to pouring my heart out to Jason? Pretty soon, he'd know everything. I walked thru the drizzling rain and soggy parking lot to my apartment building, fumbled with my keys for awhile and finally let myself through the door. I plopped down on the couch, threw my head back, and closed my eyes.

I must have dozed off because the next thing that I saw was the sun creeping through the cream colored curtains. I took a deep breath and stretched in the orange glow. I managed to pry my dry contacts out, without the assistance of a crowbar, and rubbed my itchy eyes hoping to stimulate some sort of moisture. I washed my face, put my glasses on and let my inner nerd out.

There, much better.

After brewing a cup of green tea, I sat down crossed legged on the floor and leaned against the couch. I closed my eyes and allowed the wafting scents of tea and honey to revive me. I didn't feel revived. I felt agitated.

I opened my eyes and stared at the tea bag floating around in my onyx colored coffee cup, I played and replayed what I had told Jason the night before. What had bothered me so much about last night? Perhaps it was that I hated feeling vulnerable? Or was I afraid that Jason would see the weirdness that I had come from and run to the nearest 'normal' girl for comfort? Mmmffff. . . my brain hurt. "Too much introspection," I groaned to myself.

I stood up reluctantly and meandered down the narrow hall to my bedroom. Single-handedly, I took off my red henley from the night before and pulled the cleanest looking shirt the floor had to offer, over my head. I mechanically finished getting ready, grabbed my purse and headed off to work.

Pulling into the driveway, I hopped over a few leftover puddles from last night's rain storm, and into the cream colored house. I could hear people laughing in the living room and I knew that it was going to be a good day. I spent the morning following the usual routine, get everyone up, and dressed, fed and comfortable. We watched Saturday morning cartoons and made sugar cookies. It was by all standards an easy morning, but by the end of my shift, I was ready for a nap. Preferably one that lasted for a couple of months or so. I drove home and promptly fell asleep on the couch - - again.

I swear I hadn't been sleeping that long – maybe 5 minutes, but sure enough and right on cue my roommate, Allie, came stomping into the apartment and unceremoniously dropped her shopping bags

105

onto the kitchen floor. There were some days that I absolutely

abhorred having a roommate.

This was one of those days.

We had been friends for years. We went to Jr. High

together and attended the same church all through high school. I

uttered something unintelligible and reached for the leopard spotted

blanket draped over the back of the couch. Maybe I could hide under

it and she wouldn't see me. She obviously didn't get the hint.

She plopped onto the couch and started jabbering away

about her shopping trip and a pair of jeans that she knew would be

life-changing.

"Mmmmhhh," I moaned. Allie oblivious to my REM cycle

kept chattering away and then stopped suddenly.

"So?" She asked impatiently and nudged me.

"Wha- ?" I mumbled.

"Are we going to the movies or not?" She stood up and I

could feel the couch shift.

"I dunno, I'm tired", I whined. "Just. Wanna. Sleep."

Forty-five minutes later I was standing in line with Allie and her life-changing jeans at the movie theater for the matinee. After the movie, she dropped me off at the apartment so I could go back to sleep and she took off to hang out with her boyfriend.

I dashed up the stairs to the apartment, unlocked the door, and rather ungracefully belly-flopped onto the couch. "I'm so sorry I left you. I'll never leave you again," I whispered fondly to the couch. I rolled onto my back and I laid there for a good twenty minutes with my eyes aimlessly staring at the ceiling, before I realized I wasn't going to fall back asleep. My head was too full of thoughts and questions.

"Ugggh!" I sat up and laid my head against the back of the couch. I didn't want to think about it. Irritated, I reached for the book I was reading, which I had read a million times already, on the coffee table. It felt like life in the land of 'normal' would be ending soon.

6

The Playdough Effect

The God Squeeze

I was tired, muddy, and worn out from reliving the emotional trek through several states, countries, and families.

I really wanted to stop writing.

By this point, my writing wasn't any good and sometimes not very coherent.

Remember Chapter 1?

I had mastered the art of Bleh and had moved on to Bleh 2: The Revenge.

But because I'm super-mature and realized the value of working though my childhood, I kept writing.

Ha. Ha. Ha.

Sometimes I crack me up.

Jason says I'm a nerd.

I say I'm funny.

Jason says I only think I'm funny.

Truthfully, I kept writing because I knew God wouldn't let me get away with the whole not writing thing.

God never lets me get away with anything.

I'm not exaggerating.

I get busted for the dumbest stuff.

One time, Allie and I drove under a water tower in the small

town we grew up in.

No alcohol.

No drugs.

Just being dumb.

In a small town.

Because we could.

And we almost got away with it.

Okay, so no, not really, because the only cop in this one-stop

light town followed us until we got to a friend's house. He

turned his lights on in the driveway. And we were left

explaining why we thought driving under a water tower was

fun.

Like I said, the dumbest stuff and I never get away with

anything.

Especially, where God's concerned.

So I was really hoping to stay in a normal place.

You know, I had written about my childhood, talked about it

even.

Let's forget the rest and move on.

But I felt like I HAD to keep writing.

Probably because some part of me knew that if I stopped now,

God would make me come back and finish it later. I figured

I'd better just surrender now and see this thing through.

I kept writing and talking to people I trusted, but then the lines between my writing and my talking and my past and my present all sort of collided.

And then this strange thing started happening.

My emotions began squeezing out of some weird places.

You know, kind of like Playdough when you push it through those spaghetti tubes.

I didn't know it then, but this Playdough Effect is a really good sign.

I had gotten my Playdough emotions all over my friends, my job, and my family. There were even a few pieces that had dried to my skin and were making me really itchy.

This Playdough Effect was happening all over my life.

My beautiful, normal life.

I prayed a lot during this time.

Very holy, very mature prayers – like:

Seriously? Come on. God, you can't do this to me. You can't make me write this. I don't want to. Amen.

I can't hear you. La-la-la-la. Amen.

Pleeeeaaase God, I don't want to write anymore. I hate this. Why can't I have a normal life like everyone else? It's not fair! Amen.

So now you're thinking, how is this Playdough Effect good?
I know, I wondered the same thing.

The Playdough Effect does only one thing.
It squeezes out everything burying the real you.

Pain.

Distorted images of ourselves.

Fears that God will leave us.

It squeezes everything out through tears, sometimes angry prayers, maybe a little retching if need be.

So, while it's not fun.
It is good, I promise.

God is squeezing out those things that have tried to bury you alive because he wants you to live – really live.

Remember - He ain't leaving.
He's just squeezing.

Come on, that was kind of funny.

I mean, it rhymed.

High five?

Anyone?

Anyone?

....

Sunday morning after church, Jason and I met up for coffee.
I was already seated at a high top table skimming through the
funnies, when he opened the diner door. A little brass bell rigged to
the top of the door gave a jingle, informing everyone of his arrival. I
looked up, waved him over, and laid the paper on the vacant chair
next to us. I could tell by the eager look on his face that he was ready
to pick up the story where we had left off. I was in no such mood. I

115

was still sleep deprived from two nights earlier and not at all eager to divulge anymore secrets. I was tired of explaining why I was the way I was.

Whatever way that was, I wasn't sure.

He planted a kiss on my cheek, "Hey beautiful. You miss me?"

"Not really," I said with a twisted smile.

"Ouch, that hurts," he mockingly winced as he grabbed his chest while hopping up on the chair across from me. "So, how about we order – I'm starving – and we pick up where we left off. I'm fascinated by this."

I couldn't help but twitch at his last sentence – last word, really. . ."this". I tried to hold back the mercury that was rising in my internal thermometer. But I finally understood the phrase, "she was in an Old Testament mood", as I felt my body temperature rise. I leaned back in my chair and slowly raised my left eyebrow.

"By 'this', you mean my life, right?" As soon as I said it, the dam broke. Enough already, my life wasn't some story to entertain him or anyone else for that matter.

116

"Whoa, I didn't mean-," he began, but I wasn't listening.

"I just remembered that I have this thing to do and I'm not really hungry anyways. You stay. Eat. I'll call you later." I said quickly as I held up my hand to his protests. I grabbed my purse and left Jason wondering what sort of estrogen madness he had just encountered.

After I left the diner, I drove aimlessly for an hour until I saw a cemetery out of the corner of my eye. I made a U-turn and pulled into the parking lot.

It was a small, peaceful cemetery. Idyllic even. I made my way through the tombstones until I came to one that was under an oak tree. I stopped to look at the inscription. I began to feel my throat constrict, and tears blurred my vision. I couldn't read the name on the headstone, but it didn't matter. It wasn't hers. I knew it wouldn't be, but there was always that lingering hope that closure was just a car ride away. I walked slowly back to my car and drove numbly home.

As I trudged up the steps to the front door of my apartment, I could hear Allie talking to someone on the phone. I opened the door just as she was hanging up.

"Where were you?" Allie demanded.

"I went for a drive. Glad to see you too, mom." I added icily.

Allie was taken aback and I immediately felt bad for the verbal icicle that was now shanked in her ribcage.

"I'm sorry, I shouldn't have said that." I said back-peddling. My emotions were leaking all over the place. What was happening to me?

She raised her eyebrow and said, "It's okay, but Jason has been trying to call you all day. He was worried about you."

"Sorry, I must have left my cell phone here this morning. I'll call him later." I said flatly.

"I think you should call him now," Allie's hands were on her hips and I knew there was no arguing with her.

"Alright, I'm going to get my phone right now," I said complacently as I walked towards my bedroom. I wasn't sure if I

was mad anymore. I felt . . . scared. Emotionally vulnerable.

Naked and searching for the nearest fig leaf.

I waded through the piles of clothes on the floor and grabbed

my phone from my futon where I had forgotten it this morning.

"Hmm. . . Six missed calls. Five from Jason." I thought to myself. I

crawled onto the futon and leaned against the wall as I dialed

Jason's number and waited for him to pick up. He answered on the

first ring.

"I thought maybe you had gotten into an accident. You

should have called me." Jason fired off without a "hello".

"Hi to you, too. And - - I'm sorry. I left my phone here this

morning. I forgot to bring it with." I explained.

"What happened at the diner this morning?" he probed at

my unseen wound.

"Nothing, can we talk about something else?" I replied

tersely, hoping that the pain wasn't reflected in my voice.

"No, we need to talk." Jason said firmly.

"I really don't want to talk anymore. I'm done talking." I
said sighing as I kicked my shoes off into some clothes pile in the
corner probably never to be seen from again.

*"Alright, when you're ready to talk you know where to find
me."* He said calmly.

"What's that supposed to mean?" I pulled myself away from
the wall and sat up straight.

*"You can't keep shutting people out, especially not me. If you
want to make this work, you have to open up. Call me when you're
ready."* And with that he hung up. I could tell by his tone of voice
that he wasn't mad, just disappointed. I had used up every last drop
of emotion and so, not knowing what else to do, I curled up on my
futon, closed my eyes, and fell asleep.

*My dreams were unsettling. Cloudy memories lingered just
beyond my reach. Someone was chasing me.*

*I woke up to darkness. 3 am. A streetlight shone tiny rays of
amber light into my room. I lay awake for hours, an ache in my
chest, trying to convince myself that I didn't feel a thing.*

....

For such a slow day in the shop, it was noisy. The coffee grinders whirred and aluminum carafes clanged against the espresso machine. Coffee was the best antidote I had found for clearing my head, but today, my M.C. Hazelnut was falling seriously flat.

Like a pair of deflated balloon pants.

I could hear the wanna-be doctor in my head ordering the baristas, "Push another 100 cc's of caffeine STAT! We are going to lose her, if we don't act fast!"

But I wasn't a doctor.

Sigh.

Not even one on a TV show.

I closed my eyes and tipped my head towards the backrest of the chair in an effort to stretch out the kink in my neck. I took a deep breath and opened my eyes. I watched as the brightly colored mobile, advertising the latest coffee blends, spun slowly. Maybe the truth was, that I didn't want to write. I was finding that the more I

121

wrote about my mother, caused me to face more about myself. And what I was discovering, was that my invisible walls of protection had only made me more difficult to love.

....

It was three days before I spoke to Jason. I held out mostly due to humiliation and maybe a teensy bit because I wanted him to call me first. After the third day of our show down, I realized this was a duel I was fast losing, so I bit the bullet and picked up the phone.

"How are you doing?" I said with an air of forced cheeriness. Inwardly, I kicked myself. "Was it really that hard to be honest?" I held my breath waiting for an answer, bracing myself against the disappointment if he decided to hang up.

"I thought you might call today." He said.

"Well, it was obvious that you weren't going to," I said pointedly to him . . . silently - - in my head, of course.

"Yeah, well . . ." awkward silence drowned out the unspoken words. *"I'm ready to talk. I don't want to, but I will."* I said with a note of resignation.

"Great, why don't you come on over here? We'll grab a bite to eat and then we'll talk." He said ignoring my sullen tone.

"Okay, I'll be there in a couple of minutes." I resigned myself to a long afternoon of talking about things I didn't want to.

Neither one of us mentioned my childhood or my mother during lunch. We went for a walk afterwards in a nearby park, the sun overshadowed by a rapidly darkening sky. The clouds overhead were moving swiftly and a storm was approaching. Neither one of us spoke as we walked; we were both preoccupied with our own thoughts.

I broke the silence by clearing my throat from the imaginary frog that had taken up residence in it. *"The Halberts were the first family that I stayed with that actually wanted me."* I whispered.

There I said it.

Not in so many words.

They weren't required – the meaning was implied. All of my insecurities were wrapped up in that statement. Before the Halberts, it felt as though no one wanted me.

My mother wanted me dead . . .

My dad was caught up in the demands of war. . .

The Wagners said I was "too much". . .

But the Halberts had actually wanted me to stay.

....

I groaned inwardly as I tapped my fingers lightly on the forward panels of my laptop. This was brutal on my heart and I could feel tears welling up in my eyes as I typed. I rubbed my sleeve across my eyes and glanced around hoping no one in the coffee shop saw.

I thought I was over this.

I thought this was all in the past.

But it dawned on me, as my tear ducts filled up again that I hadn't been completely healed from my childhood. I still felt like I was unwanted. Unwanted by friends, family, heck, even God didn't want me. Okay, so I was adult enough to know it wasn't true, but still. . . I had watched helplessly as all of my relationships kind of crumbled into disappointment. As painful as it was to admit, the truth had never been as obvious as it was today.

I expected people to leave because that's what they did.

What was so wrong with me, that people were always walking out of my life? Was I that unlovable? But then a man with gray hair walked into the shop and I thought about my dad. I thought about the letters he sent every week while I was in Germany. I remember, I wanted to keep each one, in case I never saw him again. The letters were reminders of the family that could have been . . . he wrote about work, the funny thing the dog did, how church was, but at the end of every letter he would write about how much he missed me.

I had been wanted.

....

"You know what your problem is?" Jason asked, as we walked to his car.

I held onto his arm tightly as I blindly stepped forward. "No. Why don't you enlighten me, Yoda?"

I heard the car doors unlock and he held my hand as I slid into the passenger seat. I felt him reach across me and buckle my seat belt. Then, I heard the car door close with a heavy thud to my right and the driver's door open moments later with a groan. Keys jingled somewhere to my left and then the car rumbled to life.

"*You worry too much,*" *I couldn't see Jason's face but I could hear the smile in his words.*

"*I don't either,*" *I said defensively and as an afterthought added,* "*Where are we going?*"

"*It's time you had some fun.*" *I heard the blinkers click in 2/4 time as the car came to a stop.*

"*Is that what they call this?*" *I muttered as I fumbled with the blindfold.*

"*Think of me as your fun guide. Today, we do what's on my itinerary and you can't argue or change the plan.*" *I felt my body lean as we turned to the right.*

"*I don't argue.*" *I said out loud to my darkened world.*

Jason snorted and then covered it up by clearing his throat.

"*Where are we going?*" *I was growing impatient and was beginning to think that this whole thing was completely asinine. I fiddled with the blindfold and could see the lights from an oncoming car bounce lightly off of the dashboard.*

"*You'll see. Hey, no peeking!*" *He barked.*

127

"Alright, alright." I resigned myself to the surprise. I hated surprises.

"Okay, we're here," he said as I heard the car engine turn off. *"You can take the blindfold off now."*

"Are you serious?" I said as I pulled the blindfold over the top of my head and sighted the brightly colored sign.

"What?! Haven't you ever been to Toys R Us on a date before?" He said winking, as he stepped out of the car.

"Gotta say, this is a first for me." I joined him in the balmy night and shook my head. *"And what do you plan on doing here?"*

"WE are going to play with the toys until we either pass out from too much fun or get kicked out by the managers," he said while taking me by the hand and dragging me into the store.

"We can't do this," I hissed at him. *"We are so gonna get kicked out of here."* I pulled on his hand as I dug my heels into the sidewalk.

"Where's your spontaneity? I used to think you were so tough."

I felt the hair on the nape of my neck bristle at the implied challenge, "I am tough," I retorted.

"Come on then. Let's go have some fun!" He said knowing that I wasn't going to back down now.

We ran up and down the aisles of the store throwing plastic balls at each other and ducking behind shelves to avoid being seen by the store managers.

"We are so gonna get kicked out of here," I thought as I peeked out from behind a metal shelf full of board games and lobbed a red ball at Jason.

....

"Okay, so that was fun." I mumbled after we exited the store.

"What was that? I couldn't hear you?" he goaded loudly.

"I said - - that was fun," my voice rose to match his.

"You're welcome," he lowered his voice and stepped closer to me as he entwined his fingers with mine.

"Where to now, Mr. Fun?" I asked skeptically.

129

"Just across the street to this quaint little eating establishment that I know of Madame." He waved his hand with a sophisticated flourish.

"You're kidding, right?" I said looking across the street.

"No ma'am, I take my fun very seriously." He said while tipping his invisible Stetson at me.

"The last time I came to one of these I was thrown out," I said sheepishly.

He turned to look at me, mouth agape. *"Who gets thrown out of a Chuck E. Cheese?"* His forehead wrinkled as he raised his eyebrows at me.

"Me. Burt and I were busted for stealing the tickets out of a machine." I winced in embarrassment. *"We had to sit for the rest of the night out in the van, while Rachel, Bradley, and Becky cashed in their tickets. I think it was the only time I ever saw Debbi get mad and she threatened to make us write 'Thou Shalt Not Steal' eight hundred times. We were both grounded."* I stared at the sidewalk as I shuffled my feet, aware this might be the lamest confession in all of history.

"Come on, you criminal. You can't have that be your last memory at Chuck E. Cheese." Jason took me by the hand and then as an afterthought added, "And hey, try not to steal the tickets this time, okay?"

....

"My mother told my dad she wanted to leave him and she flew home to South Korea. It was a loss that was bittersweet; I think . . . facing the end of anything is kind of like that. And then my dad met someone. So, I packed a suitcase and was flying home for my dad's wedding to a woman I had never met, to a sister I had never spoken to, and to a dad I wasn't sure that I would recognize." I said.

"Tell me this is where you become normal?" Jason said winking.

"You wish. Look, you wanted honesty so I don't really feel sorry for you anymore." I said shrugging. I thought back to the day I

flew "home" from Germany. A million questions raced through my

mind.

What if he didn't recognize me?

What if he forgot what I looked like?

What if he didn't want me anymore?

I panicked.

I could feel my anticipation increasing as the plane neared

Alabama. My breathing quickened. I wasn't sure that I wanted to

get off the plane when we had landed. But we did finally land and

people began to file out of their seats.

He met me at the sliding doors to the airport. He hadn't

changed; his hair was a little grayer perhaps. I hoped I still looked

the same. He seemed happy to see me and because I didn't know

what else to do, I hugged him.

He carried my luggage to the car while asking the usual

questions one asks, "How was your flight? What was the movie?

Are you happy to be home?" I must have answered all the questions correctly, because he didn't put me on the next flight back to Germany.

I felt stuck somewhere over the Atlantic that month. I wasn't in Germany but I wasn't really home with my dad either. He had a new family with Ruth Ann and Megan. They had their inside family jokes and in a couple of days everything would be official at the wedding.

"What now?" I wondered.

I was hurried to the courthouse after my dad and RuthAnn came back from their honeymoon. There wasn't much time left before I would need to board the plane to Germany and my dad would need to leave. The Army was reassigning my dad to South Korea.

I didn't understand.

RuthAnn must have sensed my confusion.

"We never intended on sending you back to Germany, Joyce. You belong with your father," she paused. Her voice softened as she continued, "I know your father is not one to express his emotions well, but he missed you more than you know. The thought that you

133

wouldn't be able to return to him, well, let's just say a part of him would have never recovered."

So, this had been the plan all along, right? Why hadn't the Halberts told me that I wasn't coming back to Germany? I just wished I wasn't always the last one to know what was going on with my life. But I kept my ten year old thoughts to myself and pasted on my best smile.

I wasn't sure what the judge would decide and I wasn't completely sure how I felt. I loved both of my families. The judge took statements from lawyers and then spoke privately with me in another room.

"Young lady, do you understand the situation well enough to tell me who you would like to live with?"

I swallowed and squeaked, "Yes," struggling to keep my voice level. Had I known at the time that I knew nothing, I might have asked for a continuance or a recess or any number of important sounding legal words to get life to slow down for a moment. Everything was moving so fast, again. There were so many questions.

And then, I heard the words come from my mouth as I silenced the ones in my head. "The Halberts are a really nice family and I like them, but I would like to live with a family of my own."

After the paperwork had been finalized and Germany was a mere memory, my clothes and other belongings were mailed to me along with letters and cards from the Halberts. I still didn't fully comprehend what had happened that day at the courthouse.

How could I have possibly told my father, who had watched out for me so protectively that I didn't want to live with him?

That wasn't true.

But on the other hand how could I tell the family that also had sacrificed so much of their lives to let me be a part of it that I didn't want to live with them?

That wasn't true either.

For the first time in my life I had people fighting for custody of me rather than trying to find a convenient place to hide me, only I didn't know it.

....

"I told you that you couldn't keep up with me in SkeeBall. Not with guns like these," he said as he flexed his right bicep and made a production of leaning over to kiss it.

"Oh man." I rolled my eyes. "Well, it was fun until your ego got in the way" I said, giving him a slight shove.

"Oh by the way, thanks for not stealing any tickets and getting me banished from Chuck E. Cheese. I really appreciate that." He winked.

"You're a jerk, you know that?" I said laughing.

He put his unkissed arm around my shoulder and gave my head a quick peck, "Did you have fun?"

I cocked my head to look up at him. "I actually did," I drew out each word, hating to admit that he was right.

"We'll get you there, baby." He said slipping his arm around my waist.

7

Moby Dick

Thar She Blows

There's a "White Whale" off the starboard bough of your story.

It's that hidden memory that you don't want to revisit.

But there's no forgetting the giant white tail that smashed your vessel and left you adrift on the sea of life. Maybe you weren't left with a peg leg, but some days it sure feels like you walk with an emotional limp because of it.

And now, you've come to the part of your story telling, that involves for you, wading through the wreckage. And it brings back memories you'd rather smother and pretend never happened.

Truth be told, it hurts.

Thoughts begin to swirl in your head as you look back on what you've written so far and you question if you'll ever really be whole again.

You wonder if there's redemption on the other side.

If it's possible for all of the brokenness, the-brokenness-you-can-now-see-so-clearly-because-some-genius-told-you-to-write-it-down, to be healed.

"Is there hope for someone like me?"

"Is healing worth fighting for?"

"What's the point?"

And the questions continue to bubble and foam around you, as you lie adrift on a water-logged board with no land in sight.

When it came to reliving some of the most painful chapters of my personal story, it took everything I had to not lay hopelessly adrift on the raft of life, refusing to feel the pain, watching the horizon rise and fall with every breath.

Not writing.

Not allowing God to heal me.

I won't lie to you.

It's hard.

It's really tempting to lay there on the raft, wondering if you've still got all of your dental work. . .

wondering if it's worth it to get back up. . .

wondering if God is really up there putting the pieces of your life together. . .

and if he is, wondering if he can do the same for your teeth.

By continuing to write, you choose faith over hopelessness.

Triumph over defeat.

Keep a cool head. Stay alert. The Devil is poised to pounce, and would like nothing better than to catch you napping. Keep your guard up. You're not the only ones plunged into these hard times. It's the same with Christians all over the world. So keep a firm grip on the faith. The suffering won't last forever. It won't be long before this generous God who has great plans for us in Christ—eternal and glorious plans they are!—will have you put together and on your feet for good. He gets the last word; yes, he does.

1 Peter 5:8-11

(The Message)

The fight isn't over and neither are you.

You still have a story in motion.

One worth living and sharing.

So maybe it's time you got up again.

You've got a fight to win.

....

Lunchtime conversations peaked and swirled around me as the smells of espressos now interwove themselves with grilled paninis. I looked up at the crowded tables.

"Are you using this chair?" an Asian woman asked me politely.

Smiling, I motioned that I didn't hear her and pulled the ear buds out of my ears. She repeated herself.

"Are you using this chair?" she asked again.

"No, go ahead," I motioned.

143

She bowed and took the chair with her.

I nestled the earphones back into my ears, bemused that the woman had bowed. A sign of respect. Did it matter to her that I was only half-Asian? I leaned against the firmness of the wooden frame of the chair, thinking about South Korea.

While we lived there, an article was published in a reputable newspaper about 'half-breeds'. It called us a waste of sperm. Most of my friends were 'half-breeds'. I was a 'half-breed'. Just one more reason for me to be classified as a societal leper.

But I didn't know just how much I was hated, until a Korean man decided to give me an education at a playground one day.

"See how far you can jump," Megan said as she pumped her legs in the air.

"You first," I said back, soaring higher and higher.

144

"I bet I can out jump you," she said with her blonde hair flying wildly behind her.

"You're on," I said back as I thrust my legs forward.

Megan flew off first and landed several feet away from the swings. I jumped second and came up short.

"Rematch?" I said.

She laughed as she walked back to her swing, "I'll still out jump you."

I raced barefoot through the sand to make it to my swing before she did, as a Korean man with his young daughter sauntered up to us.

"Leave, she swings," he said in broken English.

"No, I was here first," I said, soon realizing this was probably not the smartest thing I'd ever said. He moved quickly to the right of me and grabbed the chain attached to the swing. Before I

understood what was happening I felt the coldness of metal around my neck as the pinch of chain links clawed into my skin.

My whole body was propelled backwards as he yanked the chain toward him and my body left contact with the strip of canvas that made up the seat of the swing. My hands instinctively groped for the chain around my neck, but he was a grown man and I was twelve. It was like pitting a Chihuahua against a Pit Bull.

I gasped for air and I could feel the blood vessels in my neck and face bulge. I couldn't breathe. I couldn't scream. Tears began to well in the corners of my slanted 'half-breed' eyes. My vision began to blur and whether it was from the tears or from lack of oxygen, I'm not sure. I suddenly felt the chain go slack. I hit the ground and gasped for air. I couldn't stop the violent shaking of my hands as I wiped my arm across my eyes to clear the tears.

I heard shouting behind me and turned to see Megan going toe to toe with the pit bull who most likely would have no difficultly wrapping a chain around her neck as well. I couldn't hear what she *said; all I heard was the sound of my own breathing as I doubled over with my head hanging between my knees. I wanted to vomit.*

He and his daughter left and Megan grabbed my arm dragging me in the opposite direction. I looked over my shoulder as we ran.

My sister saved my neck that day.

Literally.

"My mother sent him," was the only thought that ran through my head as Megan and I ran.

Now, sitting in the coffee shop, I rolled my eyes at myself, knowing now that it was just an unlucky coincidence. I was merely the wrong race, in the wrong place at the wrong time.

I sighed and leaned into my laptop. I had grown up so afraid of my mother, thinking everything bad in my life somehow came back to her.

....

My dad came home from work and sat me down on the couch in our small living room.

"Your mother," he paused, clearing his throat, "Kwan-Suk," he clarified, "asked if she could see you."

I felt like I had been slammed in the chest with a fist. The air was sucked out of my lungs and a feeling of hopelessness washed over me. She found us. I didn't know how she knew that we were even in Korea, but she found us. She found me.

My dad continued and I heard him say something about the decision would be up to me. RuthAnn echoed my dad and said the decision was up to me and that they would support whatever I chose. I could feel the resignation morph into a twisted cocoon of fear. The paralyzing fear that always accompanied my mother's influence in my life.

I whispered inside myself "God, when will it end?" That night I tried to sleep, but nightmares of a dark figure breaking through the bars on our window and into my bedroom plagued my sleep.

I didn't want to leave the house. I didn't want to go to school. If my mother knew how to find my dad on a military base then I was positive she could find our apartment. How many times had I brushed shoulders with her in the street and not known it was her?

Side shops littered the streets and vendors were present on every corner, mostly selling food from portable carts. Brightly colored signs boasted the wares of the stores, although their meaning was lost on me. Everywhere people were heard bartering for better prices, negotiating, threatening to find a better deal elsewhere.

I would walk past the meat section where cuts of meat were displayed alongside of smiling pig heads and carcasses of skinned dogs at the open air markets. I wondered if she was following me. I would wander past the food into the main section of the market

where clothing, house wares, and knick-knacks were sold. Was she

one of the women I had just bought something from?

Would she know my face if she saw me?

Would she try to kill me in public?

I knew she lived just outside of this city, but I didn't know

where. I had no idea what she looked like anymore.

She was Korean.

But everyone here was Korean.

....

I never saw my mother while I was in Korea, but as we

boarded the plane to come back to the United States I silently prayed

that God would keep her alive. That he would save her from herself

until my memories had healed and my nerves were a little less

tattered, at least enough to compel me to come back and see her.

My dad retired from the Army and we moved to Minnesota,

to be closer to family. Two years passed as we acclimated to life in

the land of 10,000 lakes and a million blood-sucking mosquitoes. I

still kept a watchful eye out for my mother, knowing that she could

come at any time for me.

But then everything changed.

And as always, it was because of my mother.

....

We had picked out a simple opal ring as my engagement

ring, but it was still at the shop being sized. Jason's father, Steve,

was mildly appalled at the affront to tradition and stood at the ready

to correct his son's grave error.

"Son, you're doing it all wrong," Steve said in his most

fatherly tone. "You have to ask the girl's father first and then. . .,

now pay attention this is the important part. You take her

somewhere meaningful and get down on one knee while holding her hand in yours." By this time, Steve had gotten down on one knee and held my left hand in his.

Jason nodded solemnly as a bemused look flitted across his eyes. His hand distractedly rubbing the whiskers on his chin while leaning against the doorframe leading from the living room into the kitchen.

I sat on the faded floral patterned couch, amused by this impromptu father/son theatrical production that I was so privileged to star in . . . as the prop.

"Are you taking notes pooky?" I smiled sweetly in his direction.

"Now you try it," Steve directed Jason.

Jason was all too happy to play along with the improv. "My darling love of my life," he began while walking towards the couch.

"Yes, snookums." I added saccharinely.

"Will you do me the honor of becoming my wife?" he swiftly dipped down to one knee and held my hands in his own.

"Nothing would make me happier!" I added a backwards swoon for dramatic flair.

"Better! Now, if you only had a ring," Steve muttered as he walked off into his bedroom.

You wanna know how I know that you're the one?" I asked smiling at him.

"Tell me," Jason said as he looked over at me.

"You know that great line in that movie, you know the one where she hires the guy to be her boyfriend for her sister's wedding?" I asked.

He nodded, his eyes melting from brown to green.

"That line where the guy comes back after they've had this huge fight and he says that he'd rather fight with her than make love with anyone else. I think that's it. You know you've found the one when you find that person who you'd rather deal with the worst of who they are than be without them." I said.

He leaned in and kissed me softly, "I love you, too."

....

RuthAnn and my dad sat me down for a heart to heart in our living room.

"Do you remember Dan Sloane?" my dad asked.

"Sure, he worked with RuthAnn at the University in Korea. Why? What's up?" I asked oblivious.

"He contacted us a little while ago. . . . There was a murder. A deaf woman was murdered by a pastor and they needed help identifying the body." My dad continued in his emotionless and military precise tone.

I felt myself fidget a little as the dawn of understanding began to shed its light on the words that would follow. "Uh-huh." I nodded dumbly.

My dad didn't soften, nor did he slow in his speech. He continued like an unyielding military cadence. "They think it was your mother. We waited to tell you until they had positively identified the body. No sense in telling you if it wasn't her."

I cleared my throat, aware that I had no tears to cry. "Are you sure? I mean, how do they know that it really was her?" I said, hearing the words come out of my mouth as my brain reached out for

something to hold onto.

"Dan called us earlier and asked if there were any

birthmarks on her body that would help to identify her." RuthAnn

offered.

"Oh." I said.

"He sent us a fax confirming that the body had been

positively identified as your mother's," my dad stated holding a piece

of paper in his hand that I could only assume was the fax itself.

Right there in my dad's hand was the evidence that what he

spoke was true, and all I could think was I have to see the words for

myself. I sat stoically as he handed it to me. I didn't look at it but

instead folded the crisp, white paper in my hands while my parents

recounted the details of my mother's death. As I listened to the

details, I kept thinking that it sounded like a scene out of one of those

movies my mother had rented when I was a child.

I could feel myself shutting down.

Not thinking, not feeling.

Later, I took the piece of paper that had been faxed and brought it to my room to read alone.

How was I supposed to react?

What was the appropriate emotion that I was supposed to feel?

Sadness?

Anger?

Remorse?

I unfolded the piece of deceivingly harmless paper and began to read:

Dear Roy and RuthAnn,

Much time has passed and perhaps you are wondering if I totally forgot about contacting you again. I haven't. I had waited a long time for some word about what happened to Kim and there seems to be no one who is interested in pursuing anything about it. It is bizarre to me. It seems that the only reason for the original information being released was because folks were trying to stir up as much muck as possible about those involved in the Pyeongtaek

Orphanage scandal. Most of that has died down and the orphanage is continuing on under the leadership of the director's brother. The director is still in jail but I don't know for how long.

I've tried to get info through the pastor who originated the story, but everything seems to have just been dismissed. The pastor at the Pyeongtaek Deaf Church has closed the church downtown and has moved the church services to the orphanage site. He was the man supposedly who beat Kim to death and disposed of the body. Frankly, I can't understand the thinking of these people. One would think that such activity, even if rumors, would cause people to investigate.

The pastor from Suwon, who to whom the Pyeongtaek deacon confessed, promised to send me newspaper clippings which had Kim's obituary, but I never received anything. When I questioned him face to face, he stated he did go to a mortuary and viewed the remains of a dead deaf woman, but it was not Kim and that woman died a few weeks earlier than Kim's reported date of death. Getting info from a Korean deaf is difficult under normal circumstances but this has been ridiculous. There seems to be an undertone (unspoken-unsigned) that 'we don't go around nosing into affairs of people who might be guilty of manslaughter, especially if he has rank within the denomination and is an adopted nephew of the superintendent of the deaf denomination.

So, what can I say? I'm sorry that I have nothing to add! It seems strange that the deaf people who were doing all of the accusations during the year-long demonstration and subsequent police investigation wouldn't have taken opportunity at that time to tell the police, unless no one knew anything except the one deacon who claims to have been the eyewitness.

I trust all is well with you folk. I hear that Megan and Joyce are in a growth contest with not much difference between them. They'll be grown before you turn around, won't they? Classes started back today at the universities so I'm in the thick of it again. Is RuthAnn teaching nowdays? High School? I'll close for now and send love and prayers from the both of us. May God direct your footsteps always.

Dan and Jung Soon

It was dated August 1, 1997. My mother would have died a year ago according to the fax. Last year I was 14. I wanted to cry, but the tears wouldn't come. There was no pain, just guilt. I should have seen her when I had the chance. Why didn't I agree to see her when we were in Korea?

I carried the now creased fax in my back pocket for several days. It was my penance. A reminder that I had lost something, something that might have been in my power to save. The fax stayed in the back pocket of my jeans just as the crimson color of guilt stayed on my hands. All the while a single question forming in my mind.

Could I have changed the course of her life if I had agreed to see her?

Once again I found myself responsible for the lives of people, some whom I had never met, with a single decision of mine.

8

Rock Bottom

Where God Is

There is a place that doesn't exist on any map.

Even Captain Jack Sparrow doesn't know how to get there.

It's a place that only God can find in your story.

Rock Bottom.

He finds you and me there, wherever that may be for us.

It's a place known as desperation.

Desperation causes us to see God as he really is.

Which is good.

And kind.

And gentle.

He never throws our mistakes or hurts in our face.

He's just happy we called.

It's here in this place called Rock Bottom, where we begin to see how loved we've always been.

He never left.

In fact, God's been following us.

Keeping tabs on us.

Hoping and waiting that we will turn around and see him

there.

Is there any place I can go to avoid your Spirit?

To be out of your sight?

If I climb to the sky, you're there!

If I go underground, you're there!

If I flew on morning's wings

To the far western horizon,

You'd find me in a minute—

You're already there waiting!

Psalm 139: 7-10

(The Message)

God is here.

In your most desperate moments.

When the pain threatens to tear you apart.

It's here in Rock Bottom where your story begins to come into focus.

It's here in Rock Bottom, that we are willing to consider that maybe our ideas of God have been wrong all along.

Just like the prodigal son.

Then he said, "There was once a man who had two sons. The younger said to his father, 'Father, I want right now what's coming to me.'

So the father divided the property between them.

It wasn't long before the younger son packed his bags and left for a distant country. There, undisciplined and dissipated, he wasted everything he had.

After he had gone through all his money, there was a bad famine all through that country and he began to hurt. He signed on with a citizen there who assigned him to his fields to slop the pigs. He was so hungry he would have eaten the corncobs in the pig slop, but no one would give him any.

 That brought him to his senses.

He said, 'All those farmhands working for my father sit down to three meals a day, and here I am starving to death.

I'm going back to my father.

I'll say to him, Father, I've sinned against God, I've sinned before you; I don't deserve to be called your son. Take me

on as a hired hand.' He got right up and went home to his
father.

When he was still a long way off, his father saw him.

His heart pounding, he ran out, embraced him, and kissed
him.

The son started his speech: 'Father, I've sinned against
God, I've sinned before you; I don't deserve to be called
your son ever again.'

But the father wasn't listening.

He was calling to the servants, 'Quick. Bring a clean set of
clothes and dress him. Put the family ring on his finger
and sandals on his feet. Then get a grain-fed heifer and
roast it. We're going to feast! We're going to have a
wonderful time! My son is here—given up for dead and
now alive! Given up for lost and now found!'

And they began to have a wonderful time."

Luke 15:11-24

(The Message)

It's a gift . . . desperation.

Although, it rarely ever feels like one.

It causes us to be willing to accept something that we previously, would have never taken.

A chance to reconsider the God we thought we knew, and that he wants to be kinder to us than we ever expected.

It's a hard place to come to – Rock Bottom.

We fight against it all our lives, but life has this way of dragging us to our knees sometimes.

And it's okay – we all have those moments of desperation.

God is here – even at Rock Bottom.

....

"Mom, . . ." I began. I hesitated thinking it felt odd to be asking my mom about my mother. RuthAnn was the one who had been there for me and had done all the things that moms are supposed to.

She was the one who took me on my first roller coaster.

She was the one who taught me to drive – stick shift even, and then laughed with me as I got the station wagon stuck in the sand at the beach.

She was the one who talked me out of certain boys and steered me towards the right one.

167

She was the one who was there on my wedding day.

I had needed, not just a mother, but a mom. Someone there for me, day in and day out, through all the milestones of life.

She had been that for me.

And even though I was grown and married now, I needed her again.

"Mom, I still have the fax from Dan – the one about my mother." I inhaled a deep breath and continued, "In it, he sounds like he had called dad about a year before the fax was sent. What did he say?" I broached cautiously. I wasn't sure how she would respond to the question and I didn't want to ruin the opportunity by saying something stupid.

"You still have the fax?" I think she was a little surprised, both by my asking about my mother and that I had a piece of paper from over 8 years ago. She blinked several times, "I think he called

your dad when it happened because the police were looking for anything that could help them positively identify her body."

From there, I couldn't help it, the dam splintered and for the next hour, questions flooded out of me seeking every ounce of information that she had about my mother. The questions I couldn't bring myself to ask my dad.

"How did my dad and mother meet?"

"Where were they married?"

"Did she show signs of schizophrenia before they were married?"

"Did her condition get worse after I was born?"

"Who divorced who?"

"When?"

"Where did she go?"

In that hour, I learned more than I had my entire childhood.

They met in South Korea while my dad was stationed there during his first tour. He was stationed at Camp Humphreys and

169

ended up volunteering at a deaf orphanage. My mother helped him learn Korean sign language. They married and moved to Fort Campbell, Kentucky and a year later I was born. And then, all hell, or the schizophrenia, or whatever it was - broke loose.

That was the part I knew.

"You moved to Alaska around the time that you were two years old," my mom glanced sidelong at me before continuing. "Your mother's suicide attempts began then, along with the times that she tried to kill both your father and you."

I swallowed and chewed on my bottom lip and remembered the first time she tried to hurt herself. "Alaska was the first place that you moved in with another family.

I had forgotten, until RuthAnn mentioned them.

"Their house was on stilts," I said as I felt the corners of my mouth turn up in a slight smile as a latent memory flitted across my mind.

"It was while you were in Germany, your mother confessed to a therapist that she wanted medication to drug you. After she confessed, the therapists and your father agreed that it would be best

for your mother to return to South Korea," my mom kept her eyes on the road before her.

"I was eight, when I first moved to Germany with the Halberts. I was so afraid that she would somehow fly to Germany and find me, just to hurt me," I thought sadly, as any illusions about my mother faded into the night. I shook my head and said instead, "Is there anything else I don't know?" I asked my mom while watching the headlights from the opposite side of the highway divider blur past me.

"When we lived in Korea," she said, "your father and I were concerned that your mother might show up at your school and so we spoke with the principal to let him know that she wasn't allowed to contact you. We said that they would know her because she was deaf," my mom kept talking as my mind played with familiar images, filling in the gaps of my memories, as she spoke.

The burgundy carpet of the school hallways and the sanitizing smell of bleach came rushing back as I pictured the school secretary pausing for a moment, all the color draining from her face as the words "law suit" ran probably through her head, but much to

171

her credit she said that a deaf Korean woman had already been there at the school. The secretary had shown her the way to my classroom and left her there in the hall. As she walked by my classroom later, she noticed that the woman was still standing in the hallway. She was crying and looking through the cross-hatched window.

My mother had been watching me.

The secretary indicated to her that she would ask the teacher to bring me out into the hall, but she shook her head, "no". The secretary went on to explain that later the same day she saw the deaf woman crouched in the bushes near the buses as the students loaded up to go home.

She had been so close and I never knew.

I was thankful that we were driving home late at night, because it was dark in the van. I put my bare feet up on the passenger dashboard and rode the rest of the way in silence.

When I finally arrived home, I was exhausted. We went to bed early that night and as I laid my head on Jason's bare chest and could hear his steady heart mingled with my uneasy breaths.

"You okay?"

I blinked hard, "Uh-huh."

He propped himself up on his elbows and turned to see my face. "It's okay to not be okay."

"Yeah," I said dumbly.

His eyes searched my face but he didn't press it any further. "Come 'ere," he said and pulled me against his chest as he lay down again.

"We've been married for six months, four days, thirty-four minutes and two whole seconds," he said with his eyes closed.

I smiled and fell asleep listening to the sounds of Jason breathing.

Shadows flitted across my sleep.

A man dressed in black was chasing me.

173

I ran.

I ran until I couldn't run anymore.

He cornered me in a bathroom.

I crouched by the toilet praying he wouldn't see me.

But as I heard the footsteps on the cool tile, I knew it was too late. The bathroom was dark and humid. I waited for the door to open, staring at the light coming from under the door. The door creaked opened slowly and he stepped into the bathroom.

"Why are you trying to kill me?" my heart leaping into my throat with every syllable.

"Your mother hired me" he replied coldly.

"My mo-, that's impossible, she's dead" I said unbelieving as terror wrenched at my chest.

He cocked his head and said, "You've always known that she wasn't dead."

I gasped for air as my eyes flew open, but I lay there. I reminded myself to breathe and felt the calming sensation of my chest rising and falling with every breath. "It's just a dream, just a

174

dream." I murmured to myself, hoping to not wake Jason. I placed the heels of palms over my eyelids and pressed down.

Just breathe.

I pulled my hands away from my eyes and I slowly sat up. I shook my head, aware of the rise and fall of my chest.

I was still breathing.

....

The next day moved slowly, my brain hurt from wondering and processing all the "what-ifs". It was the messy mental hangover from the emotional overload the night before, but I couldn't stop now. I stepped out into the curtain of humidity on the front porch and took a deep breath before dialing my dad's cell phone number.

"Hey dad. How's it going?" I said trying to sound casual.

"Oh fine. What's up?" he replied. He sounded tired too.

"Um, well. . . I was wondering if you knew the names of the hospitals that my mother stayed in?" I scuffed my toe against the wood and said quickly.

175

The question he asked in return was the question I knew that everyone had wanted to ask and the question I dreaded the most.

"Why would you want to know that?"

"I –," I leaned against the wooden railing for support. "I just need to know, dad." My shoulders slumped, "I can't explain it, maybe, maybe I need closure or something," I said helplessly.

He rattled off a few hospitals and I wrote them down as he added, "I don't think you'll be able to find out much, Joyce," his voice tainted with tired resignation.

"I need to try," I said determined.

....

There was nothing more to be written.

I saved my file and closed the old laptop lid. I had crossed the threshold from my haunted childhood into the unknown of the present. I was quickly becoming a cocktail of dread and eager anticipation. Eager anticipation because I could put my mother to

176

rest and the maternal spell that she had woven over me would finally

be broken. Dread because I knew that it was improbable that my

story would close with such a clean and tidy ending.

For the next several months, I called hospitals hoping for

some sort of break in my personal investigation.

Nothing.

They were all either unable or unwilling to give information

on her.

There was always the slim possibility that she was still alive.

The police were never able to positively identify her body, as far as I

knew. A small part of me kept straining to see the future ahead,

nervously afraid that she would appear when I least expected it,

crouching behind some shrubs, ready to grab me and run.

The frustration ate at me.

And the nightmares continued.

....

"Dad, I found an old envelope that was addressed to you from the orphanage in Korea. Do you think the address is still good?" I asked searching his face for an emotion. *"I guess I feel like if I send a letter then I'm facing the fear that she could still be alive. It's closure in a sense. But what if she's still alive? She'll know how to find me."* I rambled, desperate for an ally.

"I'm fairly certain she's dead, especially with the way she was progressing." He reassured me.

"What?" I questioned, becoming more convinced that my mother was alive.

"She's probably dead." He said flatly.

I inhaled slowly, *"Okay, if she is dead, should I pay my respects, or do I continue the search for her family?"* I mused aloud.

"Joyce, she couldn't even find her family. I'm convinced that they abandoned her. I think it's what contributed to her illness." He shook his head.

"But after I refused to see her in Korea, I am obligated to do something with whatever information I find. I have to," I pressed.

"You two divorced while I was in Germany, that was your closure,
but I never got a chance to say 'good-bye'."

"Like I said, it's unlikely that she is alive, but why don't you
contact Dan Sloan from the university that RuthAnn taught at. His
wife would be able to give you information about your mother if she
has any. Your address would stay secret." He advised calmly.

"I'll think about it." I said.

. . . .

If Dan replied then it would be a way for me to keep some
anonymity, just in case . . . in case of what?

What was I so afraid of?

I tried sending an email to the webmaster at Hoseo
University, but to no avail. It was immediately sent back as spam. I
gritted my teeth and rolled my eyes. Technology can be so
dependable until you really need it.

Grrrr.

SCATTERED

I dug out the old, faded fax that Dan had sent a lifetime

ago. The words had become almost unreadable. I squinted and held

it about an inch from my face and was able to make out a fax

number.

Barely.

Not much to go on, but it was something.

....

FACSIMILE TRANSMITTAL SHEET

TO:

Professor Dan Sloan

FROM:

Joyce Ackermann

(RuthAnn Kremer's step-

daughter)

COMPANY:	DATE:
English Dept.	Spring 2007

FAX NUMBER:	TOTAL NO. OF PAGES INCLUDING COVER:
	1

SCATTERED

PHONE NUMBER: SENDER'S REFERENCE NUMBER:

RE: YOUR REFERENCE NUMBER:

Contact information

☐ URGENT   ☐ FOR REVIEW   ☐ PLEASE COMMENT   ☐ PLEASE

REPLY   ☐ PLEASE RECYCLE

NOTES/COMMENTS:

Hello,

I am trying to contact Professor Dan Sloan. He was employed at this university about 14 years ago with my step-mother, RuthAnn, in the English department. Any information on his whereabouts/contact information would be greatly appreciated.

Dan, if this fax finds you still at Hoseo I am writing looking for information on my mother (biological). I spoke with my father and we thought this may be a better option than contacting the orphanage directly. If you have any information on the details of what happened (i.e., translated newspaper clippings, details on the autopsy report, etc) I would be indebted to you. I know that this all took place so long ago, but any information would be useful to me. FYI: Everyone is doing well, RuthAnn is still teaching :) She is the high school teacher at a small Christian school in Minnesota. She would really enjoy hearing from you. My dad is still enjoying retired life from the military.

Thank you,

Joyce Ackermann

....

Dan's wife, Jung Soon, was a pastor of a deaf church. Deaf news travels fast and she might be able to find out information that I could never find on my own. She was my tiny glimmer of hope.

It was a shot in the dark. I was using the fax number listed on the fax that he sent to my family in 1996. I tried cross checking it against the Hoseo University website. No luck. So using the only fax number I knew, I tried for a week to fax my desperate attempt at

182

finding some answers. The number was almost a decade old but it

was all I had.

I tried it.

Nothing except a disconnected dial tone.

I called the Minneapolis library to see if they had copies of

The Korea Herald. It was the only Korean newspaper that I knew

of that printed their newspapers in English and Korean. Maybe I

could look through the archives to see if there was anything about my

mother's death or the protests afterwards. A woman's voice on the

other end of the line greeted me and asked, "How can I help you?"

"I'm looking for microfiche slides of the Korea Herald from

the years 1995-1997?" I said uncertainly.

"We don't carry those here and according to our database,

we don't have any archives of that newspaper in the state of

Minnesota. Let me look to see if we can have an out-of-state-library

loan it to us." I could hear her clicking away on her keyboard.

"Now you said the 'Korea Herald' correct? How do you spell that?"

"Hmmm, after all of this effort maybe I was finally getting somewhere," I thought. She took down my phone number and said that the library would contact me within 3 weeks if they were able to borrow it from another source.

I was back to playing the waiting game.

Why was I doing this?

How was it possible to feel so connected to someone I didn't even know.

....

My memories of my mother were few and I suspected about half were really conjured up from the stories I had heard. I sifted through the box where I had kept a few things of hers.

A couple of knitted blankets she made.

A Christmas card she sent when I was eight.

184

A handful of pictures and an envelope from her to my father.

. .

The address on it was from the orphanage.

I wondered if I wrote a letter, if they could tell me anything about her life. Or would my dreams prove to be a forewarning that I should have stayed away?

....

Ephpatha Deaf Orphanage

451-860 South Korea

June 15, 2007

To Whom It May Concern:

I am writing to request information regarding Kim Kwan Suk. I apologize that this letter is in English, however, I do not know anyone here in the United States who can interpret my letter into Korean for me.

185

Kim Kwan Suk was my mother and as I understand it, she passed away 12 years ago. If anyone has any information regarding her family or her life before she passed away, it would be greatly appreciated. I am aware of some of the details of her death, however, if anyone has any additional information, that too would be appreciated. She may have been known as Wansuk Kremer. I have sent along a picture to help with identifying her.

Yours truly,

Joyce Ackermann

....

I was faced with the one solution that made my stomach feel as though I had butterflies in it. I didn't want to send the letter I had written to the orphanage. I had written it more as a back-up plan and everything in me was shouting "Back-Up!" All of the possible outcomes of sending that letter ran through my mind.

What if there was still a chance that she was alive?

What if her murderer wanted to keep everything quiet now that it was years after her death?

Would I be endangering my friends and family?

Even if I hadn't listed my address, it wouldn't be difficult to find me through the postmark on the envelope. My mother had not only been mentally ill, she was psychotically dangerous. I had spent my whole life in fear of her. When I stayed with other families, I feared for their safety too. My mother had threatened anyone who had anything to do with me. That was partly why the Wagners gave me back to my father. They simply couldn't jeopardize their own family's safety. It was understandable. Why borrow trouble?

I felt sick at the thought of sending the letter.

....

It was possible that the letter would show up at the orphanage and that would be the end of it. No reply, just silence. Which would leave me in the same place I was, still looking over my shoulder.

And then there was the more likely scenario that the letter would fall into the hands of either the pastor or the director, if they were still there. Surely, the director was out of prison by now.

What would they do?

I'm sure they never considered the possibility that she had a child, let alone a daughter that would come looking for her a decade later.

My mother was dead.

Would I now be looking over my shoulder for the man who murdered her?

....

I dreamt the same dream again that night.

My mother had hired someone to kill me.

188

He chased me into a bathroom.

"Why have you come for me?" my voice was surprisingly calm, collected.

He callously replied, "Your mother hired me."

That wasn't possible, she was dead.

He answered, "Some part of you has always known that she wasn't dead."

I surfaced from my dream with a gasp.

I made my way to the bathroom and turned the cold water on full. After a few seconds of staring at myself in the mirror, I splashed the cold water over my face.

"You okay, babe?" Jason rubbed his eyes as he slid his hands around my waist.

I shook my head "no", but said, "Yeah. It was just a dream."

He frowned. "Same one about your mother?"

I nodded "yes" this time.

He leaned against me and kissed my shoulder.

189

I turned and kissed him on the cheek before walking back to bed.

As long as I was defiant, as long as I was strong, she couldn't touch me. She wouldn't hurt me as long as I was stronger than her.

I knew it as a child.

I stayed safe by pretending that I was in control.

But truthfully, I had spent my whole life looking over my shoulder. Watching for her shadow in the alley behind me or her reflection in a bus window, and because of that, I was never without her. She was everywhere to me, because I didn't know where she was. Even in Germany, I watched for her, I waited for her to come.

To come and take me away.

And still, no one knew that I was afraid.

Even here in the bathroom with the person who meant the world to me, I couldn't bring myself to admit that I was scared.

SCATTERED

I lay in bed that night, with the realization that I didn't want to be afraid anymore.

···

I walked up the stairs into the house in a haze. I opened the cupboard above the dishwasher and grabbed a blue shot glass. I studied it for a moment; rolled it between my index finger and thumb. I held it up to the solitary light above the sink. I watched unfeeling as the light bounced playfully on it's reflective surface.

How appropriate.

My shot glass and I could be blue together.

"Hmmm, you know that really wouldn't be a bad song title," I thought. I shook my head. "Numb. I am so numb. Who sends a letter to their dead mother and then makes up Country music titles? Who does that?" I ran my left hand through my hair and rolled my eyes at myself.

A friend of mine recently brought back a bottle of Jamaican rum from her vacation. I grabbed the bottle from the cupboard and poured myself a shot. I leaned against the cupboard doors and

slowly, with rum bottle in hand, slid down the door until I was

propped up between the dishwasher and the silverware drawers. I

rested my head against the dishwasher and waited for the ominous

feeling, that my world was going to change, to leave.

But the feeling stayed.

So my blue shot glass and my blue self, waited together, and

as we waited, I felt 6 years old again. The little half-Korean girl

with the big glasses and the small hands, hiding in the laundry

closet.

Afraid.

....

Jason came home from work that night to find a very sober

me, nestled between the dishwasher and cabinet, with a rum bottle

and a parched shot glass beside me.

"What's wrong?" Jason said while laying a stack of mail on the counter and suspiciously eyeing the rum bottle as if it would speak, spilling all of its secrets.

"I sent the letter to the orphanage." I mumbled looking down at my hands. Jason sat on the floor next to me.

"Hey, that's a good thing," Jason said sounding a little relieved at not only my answer but my sobriety. At least now you'll know one way or another." He paused, waiting for a response, and continued once he realized I had no comment to offer. "How much have you had?" he questioned.

"Not enough." I said sighing. "I had two shots, but I've been sitting here for a couple of hours." Jason looked a little relieved; at least his wife hadn't gone off the deep end.

Not yet anyway.

"Baby, this is a good thing." Jason reassured, pulling me towards him.

I pushed away, "You don't get it. This is not a good thing! How can I make you understand?" I could feel the anger rising. Did no one understand? I stood up and leaned against the counter continuing, "I'm not sure why I listened to you." I said glumly. I felt

my anger peak and fall, realizing nobody was to blame.

"You think she's still alive then?" Jason rose from the floor

and sat on the counter beside me.

"What have I done?" I said as tears began rolling from my

eyes. I could feel my shoulders shaking and I began to cry. I couldn't

answer his question and truthfully, he knew what I would say.

Jason wrapped me in his arms and I sputtered my fears at him,

while he continued to do his best to calm the irrational fears of his

wife.

"She will find me and then she will find you and then my

parents. You don't understand what she's capable of." I said

coughing around my now uncontrollable sobs.

"If she comes, we will deal with it." Jason said, but I could

tell from his tone of voice that he didn't believe that it was possible

that she was still alive after all of these years.

....

SCATTERED

A letter came.

It was from the library.

They couldn't track down the newspaper articles I had requested.

One more closed door.

Closure always remained just out of my grasp, some elusive ghost.

I contacted yet another hospital in Alabama.

A voicemail greeted me.

I left a message, but no reply.

Another door slammed shut.

Was this a sign?

Maybe I would never know.

Time marches on, as it always does. The summer was warm and humid. It hadn't rained in weeks. Water restrictions were in effect and lawns began to look brown and wilted. As our neighbor's grass died, so did my hunger for clarity and closure. My quest for answers lost both momentum and direction and I began to breathe a little easier despite the muggy weather.

My mother was dead.

Her murderer, a world away.

....

It was a boring and quiet Monday.

Jason was outside checking the mail. It had been weeks since I had thought about my mother. Jason came sauntering up the driveway with the mail and a wide smile that spread across his face. He thrust an envelope at me and waited for my reaction.

196

SCATTERED

The blue and red envelope had a return address from Osan, Korea.

"I don't want to open it." I said, as I held the unopened letter away from my body as if there were a snake within it. I continued walking towards the car. I sat down in the passenger seat and laid the envelope next to me. A million thoughts raced through my mind. "How ... no, who ... but why ...." I opened the letter. Two pictures fell out of the envelope onto my lap. They were both of the same woman, one of her standing, one of her sitting, both in front of a tree with delicate pink, cherry blossoms.

I knew those almond shaped eyes and olive-skinned face ... and I had never forgotten those small, child-like hands. I hurriedly opened the letter and began reading.

Disbelief swept over me and all I felt was numb.

9

Dirt Roads

Choosing God

There's a lot that I love about God.

It's not hard to love the most amazing, beautiful person ever.

It comes easy.

But one of my favorite things about God is because of something he lets me do.

He lets me choose.

For the latter part of my high school years, my family lived in a small farming town in the middle of nowhere.

Remember the water tower incident I told you about, yeah, that's the town.

It's one of those places you'd expect to see in a Norman Rockwell painting.
We had the quintessential diner, the white gazebo in the town center, even the gas station where all the high-schoolers hung out after school.

A quaint slice of hometown America, where not much ever changed.

I'm not kidding.

I remember when we got the first and only caution light in town. My best friend let out a string of expletives as we drove underneath it, looking over her shoulder to make sure that it was real.

There weren't a lot of choices as far as places to go or things to do – at least, maybe not for me.
I hear true genius needs time, space, and good music to marinate.
So I'm a bit of a loner by choice.

What we did have, were some amazing dirt roads that would wind and weave around lakes and corn fields and old barns. I think I might have made a pretty amazing pilot, but instead

200

my little blue Toyota and I tore up old dirt roads in search of choices that my former military father would approve of – you know, like ones on the ground.

Choices are like those old, dusty roads.

Each turn offering a new direction, a new course-heading for life.

I used to think God was trying to take away all of my choices and squeeze me into this narrow box of sterile Christianity.

But when I found myself in the thick of this process of writing and healing and writing some more, I began to see what God was up to.

He was healing me so that I could have more choices.

It's like it says in Deuteronomy 30:19,

I call Heaven and Earth to witness against you today: I

place before you Life and Death, Blessing and Curse.

Choose life so that you and your children will live.

(The Message)

Choose life.

So that you will live.

So that your children will live.

Not just exist, but truly live.

Writing wasn't enough anymore.

I needed to choose to live.

By choosing to be open and honest with how I felt.

Even if it was awkward and sometimes led to that awful

moment of the ugly cry.

You know, where your face gets all twisted up and goofy

looking because you've been fighting the tears for so long.

Writing was a starting point, but now I needed to choose.

I needed to choose forgiveness over hatred.

I needed to choose love over fear.

I needed to choose to believe that I could be more than just a

by-product of my childhood.

....

July 27, 2007

Dear Ms. Joyce Ackermann

203

This is my great pleasure to write to you. I am a staff psychiatrist

working in Osan Neuro-Psychiatric Hospital in Korea. Osan

Neuro-Psychiatric Hospital is a kind of mental hospital for patients

with chronic mental illness including schizophrenia, bipolar disorder

and alcoholism. I have been an attending psychiatrist for Ms. Kwan

Suk Kim since March 2007. I am writing to let you know current

health condition of Ms. Kim. Ms. Kim has suffered from two major

health problems including deaf-mute and schizophrenia. She

transferred to Osan Neuro-Psychiatric hospital from Ephpatha

Deaf Orphanage at March 1994 because of her psychotic symptoms

of schizophrenia. She transferred to Osan because of her psychotic

symptoms of schizophrenia. From my knowledge, Ms. Kim has no

family who can support her in Korea. She has been in this hospital

for 14 years.

For recent 3-4 years, generally, Ms. Kim has showed stable mood

state although she is used to complain about her auditory

hallucination from time to time. And also she is getting along with

other patients and hospital staff. Her physical condition is well except deaf-mute. However I think she needs to continue medication

for preventing relapse of her schizophrenia.

I hope that my letter can be helpful for you to understand current

status of your mother and feel free to e-mail me if you would have

any questions or comments about Ms. Kim.

Please find out attached letter of Ms. Kim and her picture.

Sincerely,

Chang-Ho Sohn M.D.

There was another letter, much smaller from my mother.

To Joyce Ackermann

Thank you for information letter.

I am deaf. So I am not good in English so do you understand me

please. I miss daughter very much. I am living in the metal hospital for 14 years. from now. because I have no home, that I want to live

in the mental hospital. please my daughter a picture send me.

Enclosed was her new address.

....

I sat expressionless in the car as Jason drove. He

periodically gave a worried glance my way but said nothing. I shook

my head in disbelief. This was not the answer I was looking for.

He parked and I silently handed Jason the letter as I got out

of the car. He began to read and I walked into a furniture store. I

looked down and could see my legs moving but I felt nothing.

I walked towards the back of the store to the bathroom. I

locked the door behind me and sat down on the lid of the toilet,

holding my head in my hands.

When I came out, Jason was standing in the hall. "You

okay? I didn't see that one coming," he said scrutinizing me with

worried eyes. His forehead furrowed with lines of concern.

206

"Uh-huh," was all I managed to mutter and I walked through the store aimlessly, my eyes unable to focus on the overly bright displays.

Later that evening, I sat re-reading the letter and I still felt . . . nothing. The enormous wave of darkness stayed suspended above me, never quite descending to claim me as its own. The truth was maybe I didn't want to feel anything, because it meant I was vulnerable. I suppressed the amber bubbles of emotion that threatened to burst against the looming backdrop of darkness. There was a glint of gold as they touched a few rays of sunlight but they were quickly smothered by the inky night of denial and disconnection.

Until whatever force held the enormity of the massive wave at bay collapsed. The dam of stuffed emotions splintered in the onslaught of tears held back for years. Blackness crashed down from above and honey tinted sea foam rose up from within.

The following week I lost it in a grocery store parking lot. Jason's older brother needed someone to watch his son on short

207

notice. Jason's parents were out of town and Jason had left work

early to make the hour drive down to get our youngest nephew.

I called Jason barely able to breathe. My hands were

shaking. "So, this is what it feels like, to lose your mind," I thought.

"I can't, I can't do this right now." My voice was cracking

and rising in pitch. "I just can't. You have to tell them we can't

watch him. Nothing can change right now. I can't do it," my voice

cracked again and there in the grocery store parking lot I sobbed.

My stomach hurt from heaving, my chest burned from gasping for

air.

What was happening to me?

"I'll call them back and tell them we can't watch him," Jason

replied with concern in his voice.

"I just can't . . . not right now." I couldn't stop crying.

Tears streamed down my face, leaving runny trails of mascara.

People were walking past my car to and from the grocery store.

"I don't care anymore," I thought as I laid my head against

the steering wheel and sobbed.

And in that unpredictable moment, in front of the grocery store, pure emotions finally buoyed to the surface. The flood waters coming out of me only increasing with intensity and volume daring to match and overcome the wave that threatened to drown me in the revelation that my mother was still very much alive.

....

That night, I tossed and turned until 3 am and somewhere between my memories and my tortured conscience, I finally fell asleep.

I saw a man's face.

Just his face this time.

But he was different from the dark, shadowy man that usually appeared in my dreams.

He had a beard and dark brown hair.

I didn't say anything, I just watched him.

He had a weathered face and kind eyes.

As I watched, his face changed.

He was in pain.

He began to weep uncontrollably, it was visceral, deep. He said nothing, there were no words to express that kind of love and that kind of pain.

He cried for my mother.

I don't know how I knew, I just knew.

I woke up and laid in bed for an hour.

I knew I had a choice before me.

I quietly spoke to the ceiling, "I need more time."

....

In the days and weeks to come I would revisit every nook and cranny of my life. I had lost everything because of this woman.

I had grown up so fast.

To survive, I had to.

I had lost my father.

210

I had lost my mother.

I had lost pets.

I had lost friends.

I had lost hope.

I had even lost my stuffed raccoon that I couldn't seem to get over, but most of all I lost a sense of security.

Would I ever feel truly safe again?

....

And with the coming of the letter, came rain. The storms raged sporadically on for days. My recently emancipated emotions stormed on for days as well. And as the rain fell heavy on the ground so did my tears, but I still couldn't bring myself to make the decision about what to do next.

....

"Now you know at least. You don't regret sending the letter do you?"

I didn't hesitate, "Yes, I do." I said forcefully. I held my head in my hands. "You don't understand. I don't know what else I can do or say to make you understand that this is not a good thing. She's inescapable. She's got nine lives or something. I mean how many people do you know that survive multiple suicide attempts and then are seemingly resurrected from a murder a decade before? She will find me and she will come. She will find me. She will find us. She may not seem capable from the letter, because of the whole language barrier thing - - but don't underestimate her. She snuck onto an Army base in Korea using an old expired ID card – in the middle of the Gulf War when security was heightened. She will come." My voice pitched upward as I ended my panicked rant.

Jason stayed quiet, not sure of what to say. How could I make him understand?

I took a deep breath to steady myself and managed to choke back any tears.

"You should come with when I tell my dad. Maybe, once you've seen his reaction you'll understand that this is not the happy reunion that you're picturing," I said lowering my voice to a whisper.

"Alright, I'll be there," was his reply.

....

It was a Tuesday morning. I woke up feeling heavy. My tongue felt like dead weight and it took several minutes before I could speak. I called my dad. "Umm, what are you doing after work today?" I asked nervously.

"Why? What did you have in mind?" he asked.

"I need to talk to you about something . . .," I could hear my voice trailing off. "How does dinner sound?" I said after clearing my throat. I absently rubbed right eye, perhaps hoping to erase the memory of the letter from my sight of my mind's eye.

"Sounds good, but can't you tell me on the phone?"

"No - - - no, I really can't" I said shaking my head.

213

"Okay, I get off at 3:30 I'll be down after that," he offered simply. I could tell the curiosity was nagging at the corners of his mind.

"Okay, see you then," I tried to sound cheery, but my words only fell dully into the receiver on my cell phone.

....

That evening, Jason, my dad, and I went to an Italian restaurant for dinner. Halfway through the artichoke dip appetizer, I broke through the small talk and slid the new, yet all too familiar envelope towards my dad. I hadn't thought of anything else since it came. I watched as he unfolded the letters and his face went white. Jason and I sat silent as he read.

My dad let out a strangled cough before speaking, "I didn't expect this. I thought you were going to ask if you could borrow my car while yours is in the shop." He paused.

I nodded my head in approval. I had no words.

214

We sat in silence for a few more seconds while we let it all

soak in.

"I don't know what to say, Joyce," he said.

"I know. What can you say?" I replied, staring at my hands

folded neatly in my lap.

"Your dreams . . ."

"I know," as I said it, I replayed the conversation with the

shadowy figure . . ., "you've always known . . . ." I shuddered a little

and looked up from the table as I was hurled back into my present

reality.

....

I tried to write but I couldn't. I had run out of words to say.

My chest still hurt. I wanted to scream or throw something, swear

and develop devastating behaviors. Anything to prove I was still

alive, that I could feel the wounds of my childhood reopening.

Instead I stayed quiet.

But the choice was always before me, so obvious.

To write her back and try to have a relationship with her or to walk away.

Hadn't I asked God for this very thing.

A chance at this?

"I need more time," I prayed. I knew I would have to face her, but I needed to heal first.   Otherwise I would place all of my blame and hurt on her, and . . . and . . . that wasn't fair either. She was as much of a victim as I was, if not more so.

I was torn once again.

On the one hand, I could write to my mother and try to foster a relationship with her. I was the only family she had. She had been abandoned. She was alone, and I knew what that bitterness could feel like. On the other hand, I couldn't easily overlook that she had attempted on several occasions to kill both myself and my father. You don't win points toward the mother of the year award for that kind of thing.

216

I spent my mornings plugged into my iPod hoping to "recharge" before my day began. I spent my evenings playing piano as a distraction. I didn't know if there was a soul out there who could relate. Even my friends and family didn't know what to say.

Was I just being melodramatic?

Was it really as bad as it seemed?

I didn't know how to feel anymore.

What were the acceptable guidelines for panic, and for God sakes, couldn't somebody write a self-help book on this?

....

"Feel something!" I demanded.

I sat before a blank screen, feeling equally as blank.

Why couldn't I feel anything?

I had come back to writing, but this time I had no words to write, no profound self-revelations. I just wanted to feel again. It had been months since the letter and I had grown numb again. This time the emotion was suspended somewhere between my throat and my heart and for some reason; it didn't want to break free.

"A caged bird content within the confines of its dwelling. I am a prisoner of my own making. I have done this to myself." I thought, cynically poetic.

When it came to emotional stuff, I didn't know much, but I knew that not feeling anything wasn't a good sign. Humans were meant to feel. It's an indication of life, like having a pulse.

But I felt nothing.

I was flat-lining.

....

Dear Ms. Ackermann

As you know, I have just limited information of past history of Ms. Kim because of lack of her informative family and her own problem with communication. However, I came to know her self-mutilating

218

behavior and violence to other persons in her past through interview

by writing. From my perspectives, her past aggression to other person

and herself would result from psychotic symptoms including

persecutory delusions and auditory hallucinations. In spite of some

residual symptoms, Ms. Kim has not shown any kinds of violence for

recent several years. And if she will keep taking medications, I think,

the risk of violent behavior would not be significant.

At the moment, I do not have any discharge plan for Ms. Kim. But I

willing let you know when she will discharge after making decision

in the future. Ms. Kim does not show any intention to visit States

and I think, practically, it would be very difficult for her to travel

abroad regarding her current status including lack of supporting

family and economic problems regardless of her opinion.

It is definitely up to your decision, but, I just want to let you know

Ms. Kim is looking for your letter.

I hope my e-mail might be helpful to you to understand what is

going on with Ms. Kim.

Sincerely

Dr. Chang

....

"Helpful?" I thought. "No, it's not helpful. I'll tell you what would be helpful. What would be helpful is if you could put a tracking device on my mother or, or . . . work with the Korean government to ban her from visiting the U.S. That would be helpful, doctor! You tell me she's violent and prone to aggression and wonder if this email is helpful?!"

After a long walk and more than a few hours had passed, I wrote a more appropriate response, sans the sarcasm, than the one I had thought up just a few hours before.

....

Dr. Chang

Thank you for the information regarding my mother. I appreciate it more than you know. I do have plans to write my mother but for now I need time to process this new information. It has been very hard to cope with my mother's situation. I was forced to live with other families as a child because of the severity of her condition. Has her family had any contact with her? When she left the U.S. she returned to Korea to search for her family whom she had not seen for many years. Thank you again and I will plan on sending a letter to her in the next couple of months.

Joyce Ackermann

···

The day after sending the email to her psychiatrist, I stayed in bed until noon and then blindly made my way to the shower. I turned the faucet on and held my hand under the steady stream of cold water. I don't know how long I stood there, staring.

I still felt. . . nothing.

I stepped into the now warm water and closed my eyes hoping that when I opened them all of my invisible scars would be washed away. Instead I looked down to see that my body was shaking. I stepped out of the shower and crumpled onto the bathroom floor in an exhausted and pathetic heap. Cold, wet, and wrapped in a towel. The tears came, but not softly. I cried violently for hours. I couldn't catch my breath and I hated hearing the sound of my own sickeningly weak cries reverberate off of the bathroom walls, so I sobbed into my towel. I muffled my agony as much as the terry cloth would permit.

After the sobs died down, I curled into the fetal position, gasping. My wet hair clung to my cheek, but I didn't move it. I laid there utterly pathetic, but unable to move. My stomach ached. I heard our dog, Savi, whimper and saw her black nose peeking from under the closed door. I crawled from the braided bathroom rug onto the linoleum and laid my cheek against the coolness it offered.

My head throbbed.

"It's time," were the only words that ran through my mind.

10

Scattered

Finding God in Your Story

Back in my familiar coffee shop.

Seems right to finish here.

This is where it started.

It's been almost a decade of writing what has now become this book.

Yeah, it's taken me that long to process everything.

Okay, fine, maybe I took a few extra years because I have a coffee problem, and finishing this book means I need to come up with another good reason to go to a coffee shop every week.

But I promise you, it's worth it.

Expensive coffee?

Definitely, yes.

But I meant taking the time to find God in your story.

It has been almost thirty years since I have seen my mother face to face.

Nineteen years since her "murder".

And it seems crazy to think, that my lost and dead mother,

has been . . .

Found.

Alive.

I don't have answers.

Most days I have more questions.

And I'm fairly certain that I'm stuck somewhere between

adulthood and a fifteen year old version of myself, suspended

in the goo of arrested development.

Gross, right?

But I have learned that it helps to write.

Even when it feels like no one understands and there are no words to express what you're feeling.

There is a safe space; it's here in the white, crisp sheets of untouched paper – waiting to help us understand our journeys.

Where we have been.

Where we are headed.

Sometimes, even a "why, God, why?" is answered.

But beyond all of that, it helps us to understand that we are still here, still very much human despite all of our scars and attempts to hide them.

And that our stories are worth being known.

First, by us.

Then by the world.

And some day, we will find that we were a bit like dandelions blown in the wind, the seeds of our stories scattered to those around us. Our words, a healing balm to others who have been wounded, as we once were.

Our pain was not wasted.

Not in the hands of God.

If we let him, he'll make it into something beautiful.

"What do you make of this? A farmer planted seed. . . . Some fell on good earth, and produced a harvest beyond his wildest dreams."

Matthew 13:3,8

(The Message)

....

I felt like I was walking into this blind. Groping my way, feeling for answers, and not entirely sure of my footing. Maybe I should get a seeing-eye dog. I looked over at my heap of a beagle on the butter colored couch, snoring and twitching in her sleep, blissfully unaware of the world around her. Savi could be my seeing eye dog, I thought tentatively. She had a lot going for her, she was loyal, dedicated, and worked cheap. On the other hand, whenever she caught the scent of a rabbit she was kinda worthless. She was more like a replacement stuffed raccoon. When I bought her from the breeder last year I cried. I was doing a lot of that these days. As a puppy, she chewed on everything and shredded the underside of our couch. She couldn't potty train to save her life and was pretty much the best, worst dog ever.

"Savi's got it so easy," I thought to myself as I blew a stray piece of hair out of my eyes. Tonight, I'm going to write to my mother but right now, I think I want to go chase after rabbits.

....

That night, I pulled out a blank piece of paper and under the glow of a lamp, I wrote my first letter to my mother.

February 20, 2008

Hello –

I am doing well.

I did get your letter and pictures. Thank you.

Jason says Hi to you too.

I hope to hear back from you soon.

Love,

Joyce

229

SCATTERED

Finding Jesus

My P.S. to You

I grew up in church.

I might have been born in one of the pews, I can't be sure.

But church is where I grew up.
And maybe where I was born.

I went to churches where Jesus was real and a palpable peace

was present when you walked through the doors.

Churches where it was easy to believe that Jesus loved . . .

deeply.

There wasn't a life that He didn't die for.

I knew this.

In my head.

And maybe some of the spaces in my heart, you know, like the

ventricles.

But something checked out later in life, you know.

The little girl who had loved Jesus, didn't really care about

much of anything for a couple of years; she was too busy

awkwardly trying to exert her independence.

But when I was 15, I found myself sitting in an old, unremarkable church, with weathered pews and a wooden cross. I was once again a little girl telling Jesus how I was sorry for leaving him out in the cold for those years.

I told Jesus that my heart had been broken from a crappy childhood.

Nothing else had fixed it.

And now I was a little wiser, and was tired of running from the pain.

I wanted to be loved again with that indescribable, feels-like-Christmas-morning-everyday kind of love.

As I said the words, my heart instantly flooded with peace and I felt him near me.
Like he was holding me.

It was that simple.

And that's the thing about Jesus.

He is the one thing in life that is simple.

He's not a complicated guy.

Not into a bunch of rules and having us stand on our heads to get his attention.

Jesus.

He is the everything we can't be.

Everything we could never be.

We can't do this thing called life without him.

And that's okay.

We were never meant to.

He wants to be our everything.

He doesn't hold it against us.

He just says come.

Come be with me.

I'll love you like you've never known love before.

I'll pick you up when you're down.

I'll be there with you cheering you on in your moments of triumph.

I'll cry with you in your moments of sadness.

I'll laugh with you in your moments of stupidity (trust me, we laugh a lot about the dumb stuff I do).

And maybe, what you're hearing now as you read this is,

I'm here.

I'm here for you.

He's trying to reach you even as you read this.

Look at it this way. If someone has a hundred sheep and one of them wanders off, doesn't he leave the ninety-nine and go after the one? And if he finds it, doesn't he make far more over it than over the ninety-nine who stay put? Your Father in heaven feels the same way. He doesn't want to lose even one of these simple believers.

Matthew 18:12

(The Message)

He's been looking for you.

Because he loves you.

Yes, you.

Maybe you're the sheep with glasses who was made fun of by the other sheep.

Or maybe you're the black sheep who always seems to wander outside of the fence.

Or maybe you're the sheep who has never really thought about Jesus, and you have just always gone with the flow of the herd.

Whatever sheep you might be, Jesus has been looking for you. And maybe . . . you've been looking for him too.

"When you come looking for me, you'll find me. Yes, when you get serious about finding me and want it more

than anything else, I'll make sure you won't be
disappointed."

Jeremiah 29:13-14
(The Message)

He's here.

And maybe you've never prayed before.

Or maybe you're a black-belt-prayer sheep.
Doesn't matter.

It all comes down to this.

Be you.

You can just talk to him like you would talk to me.

He's been waiting.

SCATTERED

Thank You

A whole lot of "thank you'" is definitely in order. There are so many people who helped me along the road to writing this book and processing my journey.

Jason, love you, pooks. You're still the one I want to fight with. Dom, Sian, & Kaiya, I'm so lucky to be your mom. I love you. Mom & Dad, thanks for letting me be me and for always being there. I am thankful for you both!! Love you. Steve & Sally, what can I say, thank you for Jason – he's the best gift you could have ever given me. Megan & Teri, I'm lucky to call you my sisters!! Halberts, thank you for being my family when I needed one. I truly appreciate all you've done for me.

Clement Vaccaro, this cover is amaz-za-zing!! You are talented through and through. Rebekah Bye, thank you for your unending words of encouragement and a very "normal" looking photo of me! Ardy McAllister, thanks for always encouraging me to write and believing that I could do it. The crew at Northtown Panera, thank you for letting me move in every week to write. Way of the Lord Church, you guys are awesome. Thanks for letting our family be a part of yours. Papa Joe, you've been a rock for our family. We wouldn't be where we are today without you.

Readers – thank you for reading and hey, I would love to hear from you. Check me out at www.joyceackermann.com. Be sure to drop me a line or two about your own story. And help spread the word on Amazon by giving this book a 5 star rating. You have no idea how many things I buy because somebody I don't know out there, gave it 5 stars.

Be one of those people, you trendsetter, you.

www.ingramcontent.com/pod-product-compliance
Lightning Source LLC
Chambersburg PA
CBHW051723040426
42447CB00008B/946